UNDERSTANDING RURAL AMERICA'S OPPORTUNITIES AND STRENGTHS

Paperback: ISBN: 978-1-64318-121-9
Hardback: ISBN: 978-1-64318-122-6
Ebook: ISBN: 978-1-64318-123-3

IMPERIUM
PUBLISHING
CREATE YOUR STORY

703 Eighth Street
Baldwin City, KS, 66006
www.imperiumpublishing.com

UNDERSTANDING RURAL AMERICA'S OPPORTUNITIES AND STRENGTHS

Edited by

Ejiro U. Osiobe

Baker University Assistant Professor
Founder & CFO of The Ane Osiobe International Foundation

IMPERIUM PUBLISHING

PREFACE

Baldwin City, located in Kansas, has great historical significance because of its connection to the Santa Fe Trail and the Battle of Blackjack, which many historians believe was the first Battle of the Civil War. The Battle involved Missourians promoting the pro-slavery ideology and Free-Staters hoping to be left alone in Kansas. Baldwin City is also home to over 4,900 citizens, one-third of whom are college students attending Baker University. Unfortunately, despite its historical significance and the university's presence, the city has experienced an economic decline in recent years. In addition, Rural population loss has long been a concern for communities across the United States. Slowing population growth rates and migration can create severe problems for rural areas and wreak havoc on their economic stability.

To mitigate these issues, this book argues for increased tourism and promotion of the city's history to address the declining trends, which could serve as a significant driver of economic growth. It also aims to identify rural communities' current and future population trends, specifically focusing on Baldwin City, Kansas. The study uses census population data to examine changes in growth rates and create population pyramids to evaluate the distribution of the population by age group. The book will identify the specific age groups which need particular attention—teenagers and young adults, millennial families, and senior citizens—and will also inform policymakers on recommendations to increase population size through retention of residents and in-migration.

Kansas is a state with various industries in the Midwest of the United States. While some sectors, such as agriculture and production, are prevalent and have been top industries since the State originated, some industries are not performing as expected. Examining the top, middle, and bottom industries in Baldwin City, KS, and Douglas County, KS, and comparing them to the State aims to see how surrounding areas are thriving and provide insights to economic development officers, policymakers, and academics in Baldwin City, Douglas County, the State of Kansas, and the United States in hopes of growing rural America from an economic standpoint.

To analyze Baldwin City's ability to attract businesses, this study uses a quantitative approach, Location Quotient, to analyze various industries in Baldwin City using employment data from 2013-2020. The findings of this study suggest that the Location Quotient is a good tool for identifying Baldwin City's strengths, weaknesses, opportunities, and threats. Through the Location Quotient analysis, the study determined that Baldwin City has four industries, Construction, Educational Services, Information, and Retail Trade, that consistently remain at basic status, even compared to the larger regions of Kansas and the United States. In addition, the following economic development strategies, but not limited to subsidized housing and infrastructure investment, were recommended via our findings.

Baldwin City, Kansas, must incorporate a business retention and expansion plan for the economy and community to thrive. Without one, businesses will not be able to get the help and support needed to continue growing and benefiting Baldwin City, Kansas. Furthermore, companies and people will continue to use surrounding areas such as Lawrence or Olathe, Kansas, rather than staying within the Baldwin City community. For this plan to be implemented, the Baldwin City, Kansas, economic development team must use the five modules. Once followed, they can apply shift-share analysis, precisely the regional competitiveness effect, to see what businesses are growing or declining compared to national employment rates. Finally, the economic development team will be able to produce attainable goals based on their collected data to retain and expand businesses in Baldwin City, Kansas.

CONTENTS

History   9

Population   29

Industry Analysis   61

Business Attraction   89

Business Retention   107

HISTORY

Authors: Ejiro U. Osiobe and Tristen Quillen

BALDWIN CITY is in Kansas between Ottawa City, Kansas (KS) and Lawrence City, KS. Baldwin is approximately 40 miles southeast of Topeka, KS, and 36 miles southwest of Overland Park, KS [1]. Baldwin is a unique city with great historical riches, including the Blackjack Battlefield, the Maple Leaf Festival, and Baker University. As of the 2020 census, the population of Baldwin is home to over 4,900 citizens living in Kansas. One-third of those residents are college students attending Baker University, historically known in Kansas as the #1 ranked business and economics department and the oldest university in Kansas. Baker University is the city's backbone because the university is the community's major employer, bringing in much attraction, including but not limited to talents, students, and (inter)national business activities towards the Baldwin community. Unfortunately, the city has experienced economic loss for the past few years, with a 3.97% decline in employment [from 2.19k to 2.11k] in 2020 [2].

Downtown Baldwin City, Kansas

This chapter seeks to cover the historical events within Baldwin and what ultimately led to the creation of the city. Baldwin City is relatively like

Louisburg and Edwardsville as it sits west and south of the two cities, ranking at #65 on the Kansas population scale [3]. The town's size is no big capital, but the city is not something a person can drive through as if it were a ghost town. The history of Baldwin is not highlighted enough throughout the city in a way that may attract some tourism communities outside the town seeking historical knowledge. This chapter aims to address the issue of

Figure 1:
A Map Showing the Outline of Baldwin City

[1]

economic decline in Baldwin City, Kansas, despite its notable history and the presence of a four-year University. Despite being home to the Battle of

Blackjack, the Santa Fe Trail, and the Maple Leaf Festival, the city has been experiencing a decline in employment, with a 3.97% drop in 2020 [3]. The primary focus of this chapter is to advocate for an increase in tourism and the

Figure 2:
Baldwin Location Inside Kansas and Country

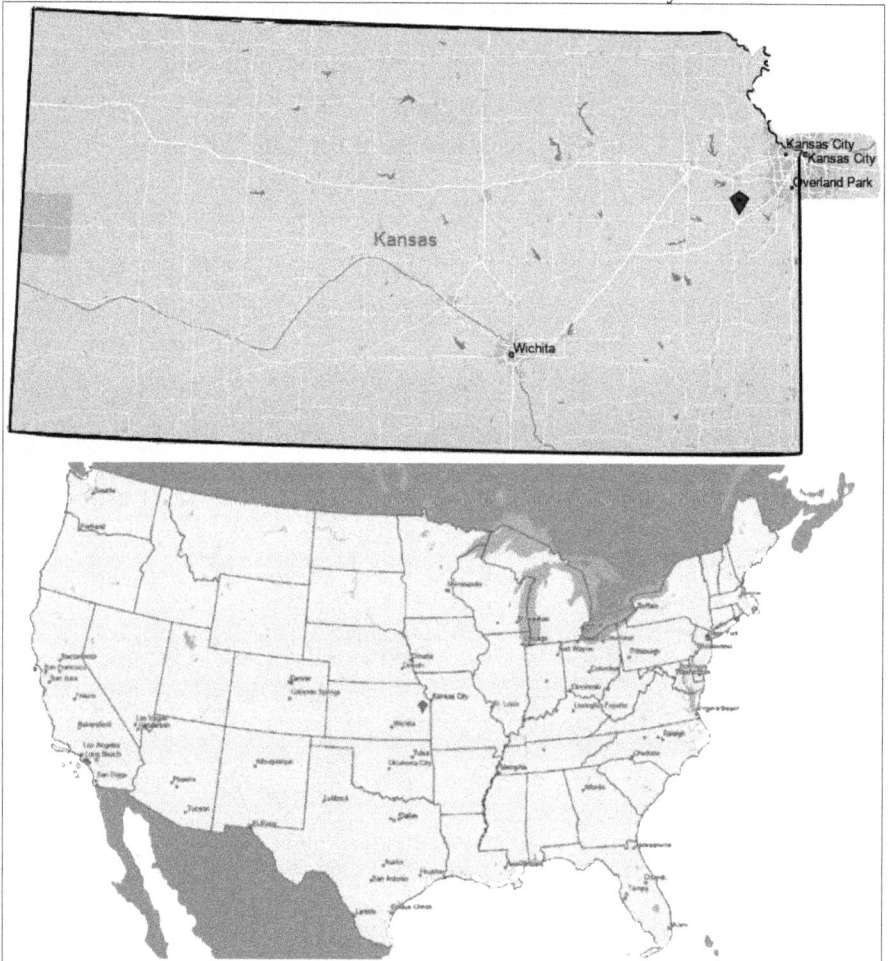

[1]

promotion of the city's history as a significant driver of economic growth. Baldwin City has a rich history, particularly its connection to the Santa Fe

Trail and the Battle of Blackjack [4], which makes it a desirable location for tourists interested in historical knowledge. The Santa Fe Trail was used during the Mexican American War to invade New Mexico in 1846 and became a trade route for the gold rush in Colorado and California in 1848 [4]. The Battle of Blackjack in 1856 marked a turning point in United States history by demonstrating antislavery sentiment against pro-slavery. The paper suggests that highlighting the city's rich history could attract more tourists, boosting the city's economy [5].

The historical trail of Baldwin City leads as far back as the trail of Santa Fe, which is commonly known for the many impacts it had on America's history. The Santa Fe Trail is also known for the creation of Baldwin on May 30, 1854, where white settlement began [6]. The legislation known as the Kansas-Nebraska Act of 1854, encompassing the present-day

Figure 3:
Picture Location of The Battle of Blackjack (archival photo)

[5]

states of Kansas, Nebraska, Montana, and the Dakotas, was initially referred to as a bill "to organize the Territory of Nebraska" [7]. Despite its initial label, people at the time commonly called it "the Nebraska Bill." In which the land became a zone for voting to decide on being a free or enslaved person state [8]. This act pulled in many settlers from out of state into Kansas. This ultimately ignited a settlement that Robert and Richard Pearson first established in the area where the city of Baldwin was established.

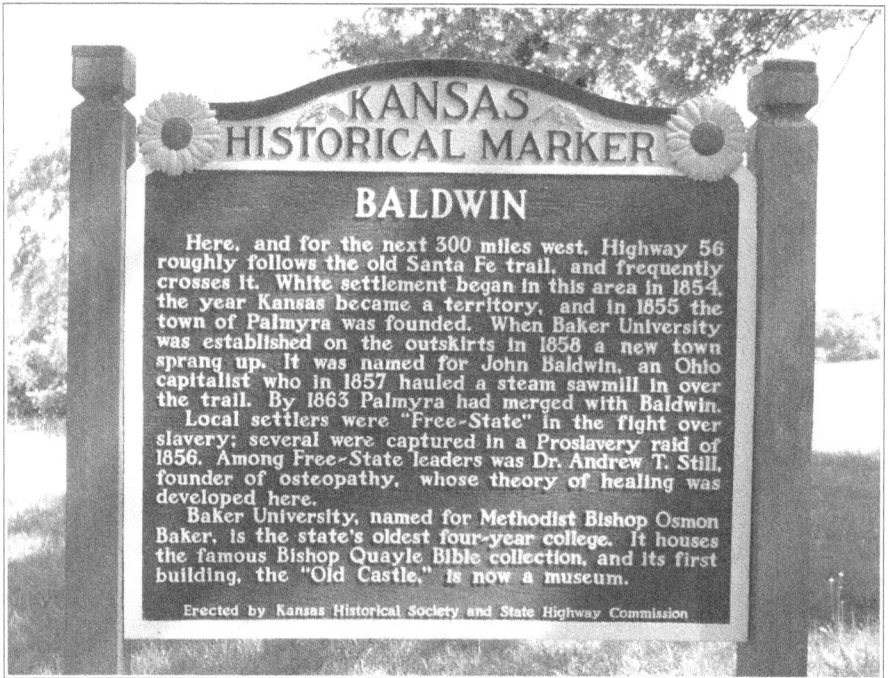

Historical marker east of Baldwin City

The migration of people flowing from the Santa Fe Trail into Palmyra is essential to establishing Baldwin City. This trail not only brought in the economic growth of currency from outside Palmyra but also produced more settlers to populate the future of Baldwin City [9]. In 1856, the Battle of Blackjack occurred 3 miles east of Palmyra; many historians argue it was the first Battle of the Civil War [10]. The Battle of Blackjack was a "watershed moment in the United States history" [11]. It proved to be a strong statement towards antislavery in the country fighting back against pro-slavery. The Battle involved two groups, Missourians, who were pro-slavery

Marker at the site of the pre-Civil War battle of Black Jack

at the time as these people were constantly invading Kansas to promote their pro-slavery ideology. These pro-slavery ideologues ultimately created the Kansas group of "Free-Staters." This group was living in Kansas, hoping to be left alone. A major strike by the pro-slavery group was the sack of Lawrence on May 21, 1856. Samuel Jones, a county sheriff for Douglass County, marched 900 pro-slavers to Lawrence. In Lawrence, they looted most of the town, destroyed two printing presses, and burned down a free state hotel [11]. Onward with the sacking of Lawrence, the free staters had to endure another horrific event with the caning of Republican and abolitionist United States (US) senator from Massachusetts, Charles Sumner [11]. Free-Stater abolitionist John Brown gathered many other free staters like him, including his sons, and marched down to Pottawatomie Creek in Franklin County, Kansas [11]. At Franklin County, the free states shocked the whole nation with their actions as they hacked five pro-slavery settlers apart by using broadswords.

An historic cabin on the site of the Black Jack battlefield

The Santa Fe trail running through the area of Baldwin is where the Battle began as the Free Staters took them by surprise upon the pro-slavery group's arrival. Brown and his men took position by the gullies on the Santa Fe Trail, and Samuel took charge, coming at a downhill attack. The Free Staters had a more strategic advantage with their position, ultimately deceiving Pate and his pro-slavers. Brown and Pate drew up an "Article of Agreement" to end the conflict and settle the Battle for the two parties battling [11]. This "Article of Agreement" acted out as a prisoner exchange. Brown received his two sons back; Pate was let go along with his second in command [11]. The Battle of Blackjack ultimately set the course as it's debated to be the first Battle leading into the Civil War and with the bleeding of Kansas. After the Battle, Robert Pearson purchased over 200 plus acres of land from Wyandot Indians, which also involved the purchase of the Blackjack battlefield.

John Baldwin, an American Methodist minister, a Baldwin native, and an educator, established Baker University in 1858, giving the institution

Old Castle Museum - the stone building on the right

Osmon Cleander Baker's name in honor of the Methodist bishop. The school is recognized for having been the first four-year university in Kansas. Baker

Parmenter Hall, the oldest university building still in active use

University later implemented its School for Professional and Graduate Studies (SPGS) in 1988 and 1991 when they joined a joint contract with Stormont-Vail Regional Medical Center. Lastly, in more recent years, in 2005, the School of Education was established in Baker [12]. It is still connected to the United Methodist Church and is currently the oldest university in Kansas [6].

Baker University's first stone building, the Old Castle Hall, opened its doors in 1858. This historic structure is now known as the Old Castle Museum (open by appointment only) and may be found a block east of the Baldwin City campus. The Old Castle was Baker University's primary facility for many years, housing a chapel, administration offices, classrooms, and even a library. Today, it holds artifacts from Baker and the surrounding community's history.

In 1866, Abraham Lincoln donated funds to build the second permanent building on campus—Parmenter Hall—with its distinctive Gothic architecture and stained-glass windows. Parmenter Hall is still a part of Baker University's campus today, serving several roles such as offices, event space, and classes. Its distinctive characteristics and legacy have made it a revered symbol of the university's history. It is even on the National Register of Historic Places.

The Baldwin State Bank was founded in 1892 [8]. Baldwin State Bank, one of Kansas's original banks, has its roots in the foundation of Baldwin City. A group of local businesses recognized the need for a trustworthy banking institution in the growing town. Baldwin State Bank began as a small community bank, providing residents and businesses with essential financial services. The bank has been through many ups and downs, including the Great Depression.

Baldwin State Bank before the facade was modernized (archival photo)

On April 5, 1889, Mayor Lucy Sweet Sullivan and all women's city council were elected. [10]. American suffragist and political activist Lucy

The Women's Bridge initially constructed during Lucy Sullivan's tenure as mayor

Sweet Sullivan contributed to the cause of women's suffrage in Kansas and the rest of the country. She also significantly impacted the Kansas State Suffrage Amendment, passed in 1912, and gave Kansas women the right to vote in federal and state elections. Sullivan was a tireless worker for women's suffrage and a fervent supporter of temperance.

Lumberyard Arts Center (the historic Ives-Hartley Building)

The Lumberyard Arts Center, a community gallery and regional arts hub, is housed in the former Ives-Hartley Lumber Company Building. The 108-over-year-old structure has housed several retail businesses over the years besides lumber [6]. The Ives-Hartley Lumber Company building is a landmark stop in the heart of Baldwin City, Kansas. It was constructed in 1914 and functioned as the Ives–Hartley Lumber Company, providing lumber and building supplies to the community. The building is distinguished by a red brick facade with a window grid highlighting the structure's verticality. The current layout of the front half of the building features a sizable open courtyard, classrooms, a catering kitchen, gallery space, and an office. The back half of the building is still in its original state, waiting for

The Lumberyard Arts Center courtyard and event space

funding to turn the space into a live theater. The Ives-Hartley Lumber Company building is now recognized as a significant piece of Baldwin City's architectural history and has hit its 100th anniversary as a downtown landmark [13].

The Liston Stadium is located within the city of Baldwin, a sports stadium owned and operated by Baker University. It was named after John F. Liston, a former football coach and athletic director at Baker University who recognized the need for a suitable sports facility on campus. The stadium construction began in 1927 and was completed 1928 at $25,000 [14].

Liston Stadium: photo © Masterbloseph posted on Kansas High School Athletics Wiki

Initially, it had a seating capacity of 6,000, but it has undergone numerous restorations and additions to accommodate over 10,000 people. The Stadium has hosted numerous sporting events and community activities, that includes football, soccer, track & field tournaments, graduations, and concerts. Both Baker University and the city of Baldwin's history can be traced back to

Liston Stadium. Baker students and alums constructed the building during difficult economic times [15], and its completion demonstrated the community's perseverance and spirit. The Stadium has been a setting for various games and local area exercises, making it a cherished milestone in Baldwin City. Baker University's alums can help in multiple ways, such as donating money for stadium renovations and upgrades. Baker University's athletic programs and Liston Stadium have the potential to benefit Baldwin. Visitors can help the local economy by using the Stadium for community and sporting events. In addition, the college and its athletic projects add to the city's social texture and give unique open doors for inhabitants to meet up and celebrate. Liston Stadium is a beloved Baldwin City landmark and an important part of Baker University's history. Baker's athletic programs have been successful due to improvements and renovations to the Stadium funded by alum contributions [14]. Moreover, the Stadium and athletic projects can affect the city socially and financially.

BALDWIN CITY MAPLE LEAF FESTIVAL

Baldwin City hosts the Maple Leaf Festival every year to honor the passing of the seasons and the town's illustrious past. The festival's first iteration, which took place one day in the fall to synchronize with the maple leaves changing hues, dates back to 1958. The festival became a multi-day event with a parade, artisan market, car show, live music, and other attractions as it grew in popularity. Currently, with tens of thousands of attendees each year, the Maple Leaf Festival is one of the most significant occasions in the area. The festival has a solid connection to Baldwin City's past and present. For several reasons, the Maple Leaf Festival is essential to the community and the region. First, it significantly boosts the local

Maple Leaf Festival, the third full weekend in October

economy, as thousands of visitors flock to Baldwin City during the festival to enjoy the festivities and patronize local businesses. This increased tourism and spending helps support the town's small businesses and creates jobs for residents. The maple leaf was selected as the festival's emblem because there are so many maple trees in the area. The Maple Leaf Festival commemorates the change of seasons and honors local culture and history. It allows locals to unite and celebrate their shared history and culture while welcoming guests from nearby to enjoy Baldwin City's distinctive charm.

One method the city can use to advance tourism is to make a website highlighting the city's attractions, counting chronicled points of interest, neighborhood celebrations, and occasions. The site can be planned to target sightseers, both domestic and universal, who are curious about history,

Baldwin City train depot, at one time host to *Thomas the Train* and *Polar Express*

culture, and uniqueness. The city can make guided visits to authentic areas that peak concerns out of curiosity, counting the Santa Fe Trail and the location of the Battle of Blackjack. Local historians can conduct the holidays and give bits of knowledge about the events throughout the city. Baker University can offer courses that center on the city's history and culture, drawing in more understudies to the college and the city. To attract more businesses, the neighborhood government can offer charge motivating forces and endowments to companies that contribute within the town. Lastly, the city can make a business-friendly environment by streamlining the method of getting grants and licenses through local universities.

CONCLUSION

In closing, advancing the city's history and culture through tourism and organizations can help the town of Baldwin to overcome its financial decrease and create new openings for development. The City of Baldwin in Kansas is a unique and historical city home to over 4,900 citizens, with one-third of college students attending Baker University. Unfortunately, the city's rich history is not expanded or promoted enough to attract tourism communities outside the town seeking historical knowledge. The historical trail of Baldwin City leads back to the Santa Fe Trail, which ultimately led to the creation of Baldwin City on May 30, 1854. The Battle of Blackjack, three miles east of Palmyra, was significant in American history. It proved to be a strong statement towards antislavery in the country fighting back against pro-slavery. The city's backbone is Baker University, the community's major employer, bringing talents, students, and (inter)national business activities to the Baldwin community. Despite experiencing economic loss for the past few years, Baldwin City remains a hidden gem worth exploring.

REFERENCES

[1] "On The Map," United States Census Bureau, 27 3 2023. [Online]. Available: https://onthemap.ces.census.gov/. [Accessed 27 3 2023].

[2] IPEDS, OPE Accreditation, OPE security, OPE Athletics, Unsplash, "College Tuition Compare," 2023 College Tuition Compare, 2022. [Online]. Available: https://www.collegetuitioncompare.com/edu/168847/baker-college/enrollment/. [Accessed 27 3 2023].

[3] Census Bearue, "Data USA: Baldwin City, KS," Deloitte, Datawheel, Cesar Hidalgo, 2020. [Online]. Available: https://embed.datausa.io/profile/geo/baldwin-city-ks/. [Accessed 27 3 2023].

[4] Santa Fe SOAP Ranch, "Santa Fe SOAP Ranch," Santa Fe Soap Ranch. POS and E-commerce by Shopify., 11 6 2021. [Online]. Available: https://www.santafesoapranch.com/blogs/news/the-santa-fe-trail#:~:text=In %201846%2C%20the%20American%20army,during%20th e%20Mexican%2DAmerican%20War. [Accessed 1 5 2023].

[5] Kansas State Agency, "Kansapedia Kansas Historical Society," Kansas Historical Society, 6 2103. [Online]. Available: https://www.kshs.org/kansapedia/battle-of-black-jack/18315. [Accessed 1 5 2023].

[6] Baldwin City, Baldwin City, Kansas: History, Baldwin City, 2023.

[7] Senate Government, "The Kansas-Nebraska Act," 1 5 2023. [Online]. Available: https://www.senate.gov/artandhistory/history/minute/Kansas_Nebraska_Act.htm#:~:t ext=Ostensibly%20a%20bill%20"to%20organize,Kansas%2DNebraska%20Act %20of%201854.. [Accessed 1 5 2023].

[8] "LJWorld.com," Syncronex, 2023. [Online]. Available: https://www2.ljworld.com/news/general-] news/2022/aug/27/baldwin-city-and-eudora-wont-raise-property-tax-rates-for-2023-but-tax-bills-arent-likely-to-shrink/ #:~:text=In%20Baldwin%20City%2C%20City%20Administrator, the%20city%20%241%2C028%20in%20taxes. [Accessed 27 3 2023].

POPULATION

Authors: Ejiro U. Osiobe and Emmerth L. Joseph

BALDWIN CITY, Kansas (KS), is a rural town with a slow population growth in the past ten years. Baldwin City is thirty-three miles northwest of the capital city of Topeka, KS, and currently has a population of 4,900. Historical migration to Baldwin City was determined by its place along the Santa Fe Trail, a popular trade route during the Gold Rush of the 1840s and 1850s. Baldwin City's current population trends are greatly affected by Baker University, the community's major employer and home to many college residents (Osiobe & Quillen, 2023).

Government officials must know their population growth trends and the breakdown of the most affected age groups to continue Baldwin City's development. The economic stability of a rural community such as Baldwin City is greatly affected by a loss in population size. This chapter argues that addressing concerns within the age groups that are opportunities for growth in Baldwin City will increase the community's population and economic vitality.

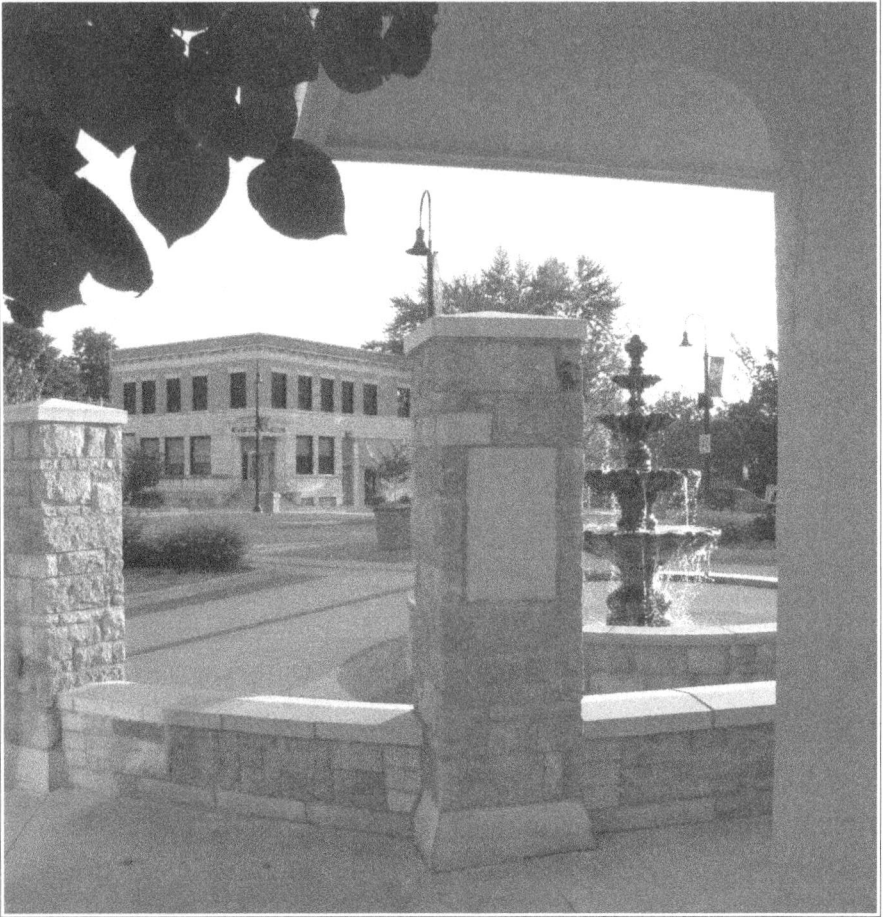
The heart of the downtown business district with a view of City Hall

CHRONICLES

Marre (2020) states that rural areas with population loss or slow growth face problems like a shrinking workforce and tax base and an aging population with needs that pressure rustic healthcare options. He asserts that historically, rural communities have been able to compensate for things like urbanization and population loss through natural increases or fertility rates.

However, Marre argues that with fertility rates trending downward, rural communities must consider reducing out-migration and increasing in-migration as the best way to combat population decline. He gives multiple strategies for bringing new residents to rural communities. Still, most revolve around encouraging young adults to stay in the community and attracting middle-aged and older adults. In addition, he emphasizes the need for quality

Baker University Student Union

public schooling, linking high school and college students with local career opportunities, and expanding broadband access.

Fiore et al. (2015) focus on brain drain, which is the out-migration of college-educated individuals. The study gathered survey data from public college graduating seniors in rural Iowa. The survey included a comprehensive list of factors that might affect these seniors' migration patterns. Fiore et al. found that the respondents felt that the overall cost of living and a robust local economy were the top-ranked features in their migration decisions. Based on these findings, the study also discusses implementations for policymakers to consider, such as connecting rural economies with local higher education institutions.

THE CITY'S POPULATION SIZE

Baldwin City, currently sitting at a population size of 4,900, has seen slow population growth. Over the past twenty years, the population percentage change growth rate averaged 1.2%. Over the past ten years, Baldwin City's percentage change growth rate slowed even more to an average of 0.54%. While the growth rate has not dipped into negative territory within the last ten years, the city is still operating at too low of a growth rate for any substantial growth in population size (US Census Bureau, 2023). Figure 1 shows spikes in the percentage change in population growth surrounding 2000, 2010, and 2020. Given that these are US population census collection years, the data will be slightly skewed from non-census years, leading to sudden spikes in growth percentage change.

COMPARATIVE GROWTH RATES

Comparing Baldwin City's population growth to that of the state of Kansas, the surrounding Midwest area and the United States provides a holistic understanding of Baldwin City's population growth. Figure 2 shows us that Baldwin City has had a percentage change in growth near the level of or better than these areas. Once again, Baldwin City's ten-year average percentage change in growth is 0.54%. The Midwest region has a 0.32% 10-year average percentage change in growth, while the state of Kansas has a 0.19% 10-year average change in growth. The only area outperforming Baldwin City is the United States at a 10-year average percentage change of 0.59% (US Census Bureau, 2023). It is reassuring to see that Baldwin City has a higher population growth rate on average than the areas that encompass the town. However, it is essential to note that while these are positive numbers, they are still too small to pursue significant growth in Baldwin City.

Figure 1:
Baldwin City Percentage Change in Population Growth
(2000-2021)

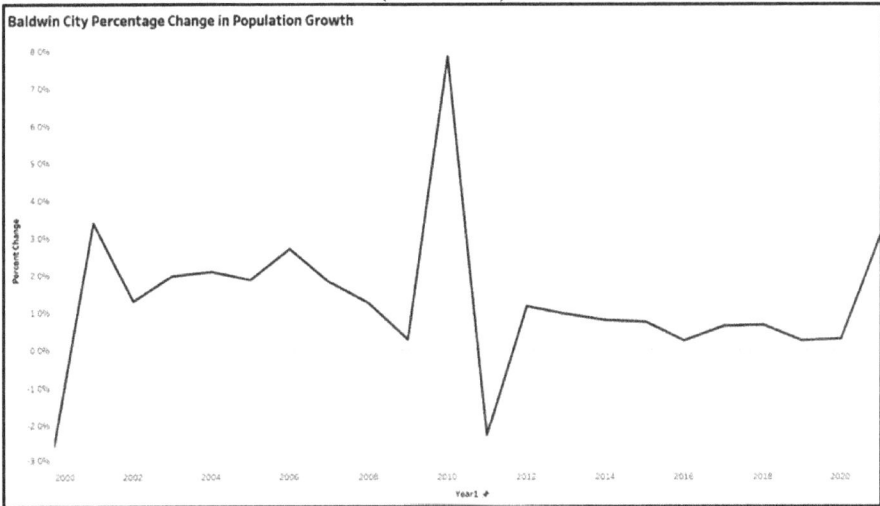

Source: U.S. Census Bureau (2023)

PROJECTED GROWTH RATES

While the population growth rate has been relatively minimal in the last five years, the level has remained consistent. However, based on forecasted estimations, the growth rate will decrease slightly and level out with other surrounding areas moving forward.

Figure 2:
Population Percentage Change (2012-2021)

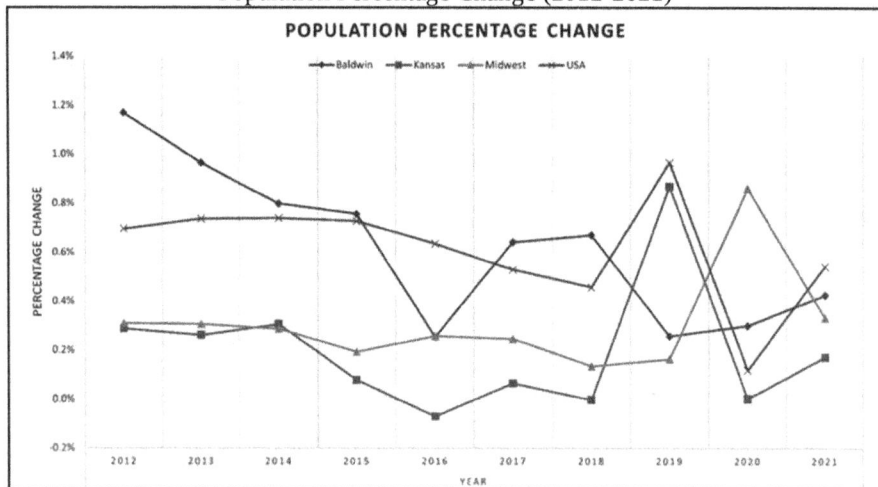

Source: U.S. Census Bureau (2023)

FORECASTING MODEL

The first-order equation:

$$Y_t = \alpha + \delta_t + \varepsilon_i \dots \dots \dots \dots \dots (1)$$

Where:

Y_t = Known years population.

α = Constant within the model.

δ_t = Timeseries – time trend accounting for both known and unknown populations.

ε_i = Error term within the model.

The nth–order equation:

$$Y_t = \alpha + \delta_n t + \delta_n t^n + \varepsilon_i \dots \dots \dots (2)$$

Figure 3:
Projected Population Growth Rate (2024-2035)

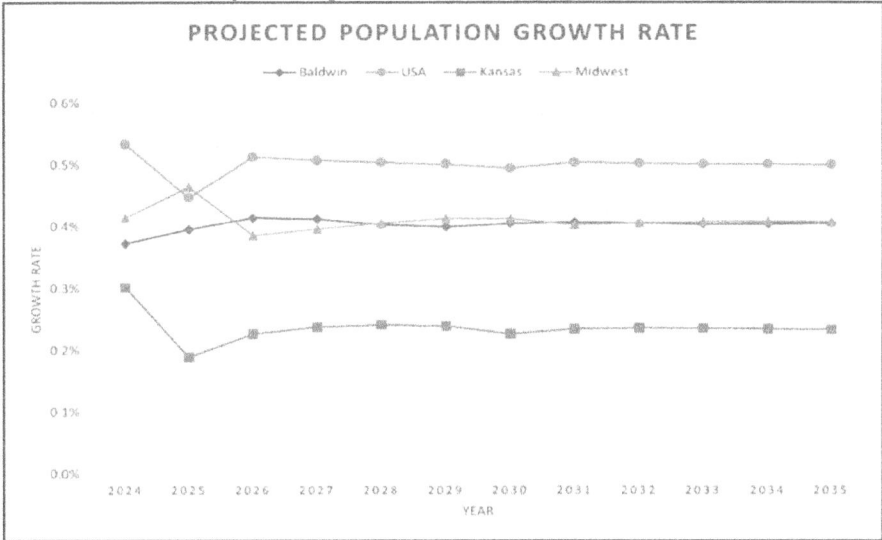

Source: Authors Calculation (2023)

Figure 3 showcases the projected growth rates till 2035 for Baldwin City, the Midwest, Kansas, and the United States. Projection techniques cause each growth rate to eventually even out, but these can be used as a valid estimate of the expected rates in the future. For example, Baldwin City's projected population growth rate for about the next ten years is about 0.4% which is right on par with the Midwest, which has a similar estimate (US Census Bureau, 2023).

Baldwin City is looking at an almost doubled rate of growth compared to the state of Kansas, which has a projected average growth rate of 0.23% over the next ten years. The United States will continue to grow slightly more than Baldwin City, with a projected growth rate of 0.5% average over the next ten years. A projected growth rate above that of the state of Kansas and similar to the Midwest is a good sign for Baldwin City to be able to maintain its population size and reduce the risk of a declining population shortly. However, a growth rate of 0.4% for the next ten years will not support the desired level of expansion and development of Baldwin City.

POPULATION PYRAMIDS

The most recent US Census from 2020 provides the most accurate data points for evaluating the breakdown of age demographics. Therefore,

Figure 4:
Population Cohort Pyramid Structure of Baldwin City, Douglas County, and The United States (2020)

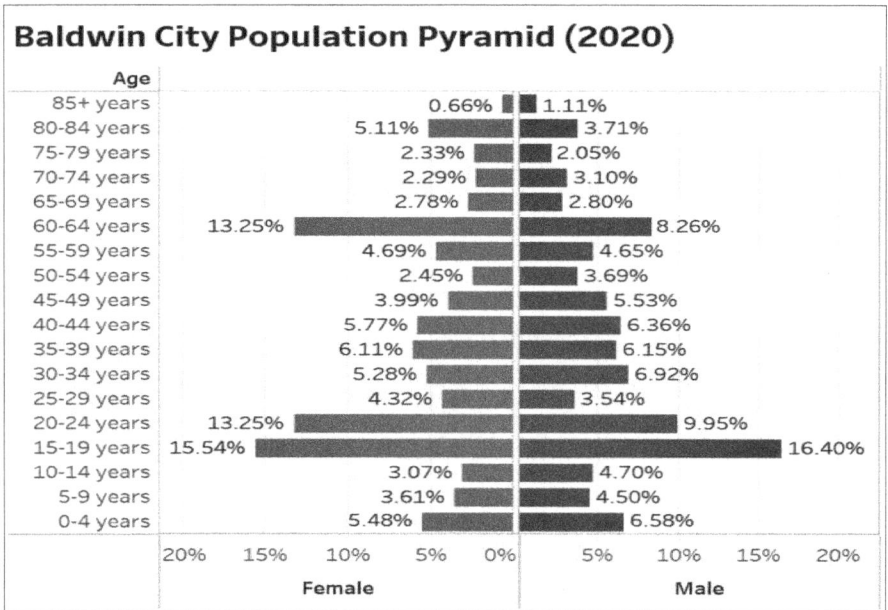

Baldwin City Population Pyramid (2020)

population data cohorts from 2020 will be shown as a pyramid for Baldwin City, Douglas County, and the United States. Figure 4 showcases the severe

Figure 4 (cont.):

Douglas County Population Pyramid (2020)

Age	Female	Male
85+ years	2.90%	1.60%
80-84 years	2.20%	1.50%
75-79 years	2.90%	2.40%
70-74 years	4.00%	3.50%
65-69 years	5.40%	5.20%
60-64 years	6.50%	6.10%
55-59 years	6.60%	6.40%
50-54 years	5.90%	5.90%
45-49 years	5.60%	5.80%
40-44 years	5.80%	5.90%
35-39 years	6.30%	6.60%
30-34 years	6.40%	6.60%
25-29 years	6.40%	7.00%
20-24 years	6.90%	7.70%
15-19 years	6.70%	7.10%
10-14 years	6.70%	7.00%
5-9 years	6.60%	7.00%
0-4 years	6.30%	6.70%

US Population Pyramid (2020)

Age	Female	Male
85+ years	2.60%	1.50%
80-84 years	2.10%	1.60%
75-79 years	3.00%	2.50%
70-74 years	4.30%	3.80%
65-69 years	5.50%	5.10%
60-64 years	6.40%	6.10%
55-59 years	6.80%	6.60%
50-54 years	6.40%	6.40%
45-49 years	6.30%	6.30%
40-44 years	6.10%	6.20%
35-39 years	6.40%	6.60%
30-34 years	6.60%	7.00%
25-29 years	6.90%	7.40%
20-24 years	6.40%	7.00%
15-19 years	6.20%	6.70%
10-14 years	6.20%	6.70%
5-9 years	5.90%	6.30%
0-5 years	5.80%	6.30%

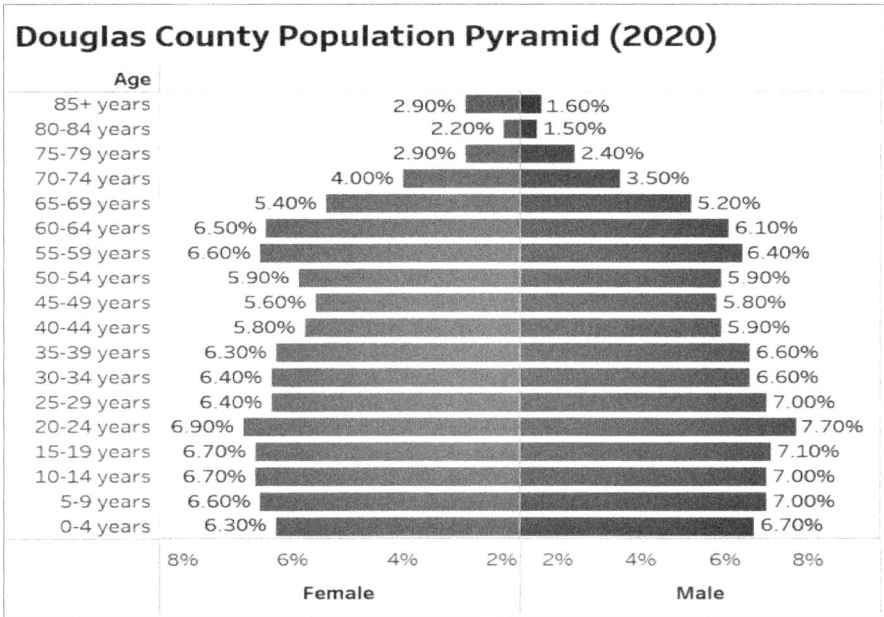

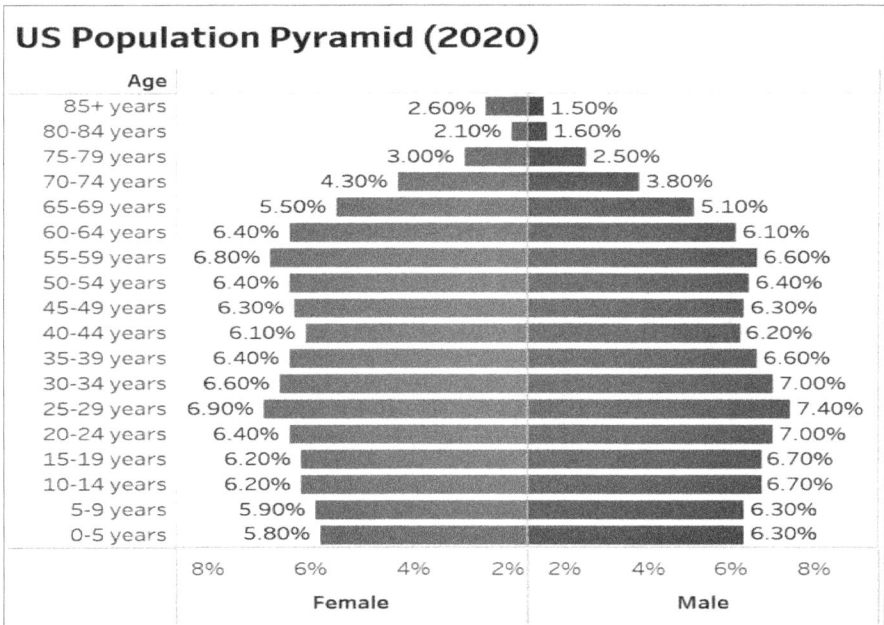

Source: U.S. Census Bureau (2023)

problems with Baldwin City's age demographics; there is uneven distribution, especially when compared to healthier population pyramids such as Douglas County and the United States in 2020 (US Census Bureau, 2023).

Figure 5 shows a projection of Baldwin City's population pyramid in 2030 based on our forecasting model (see equations 1 & 2). The population appears to be continuing its current path of uneven distribution of age demographics, just in a more extreme manner. Based on these estimations, there is serious concern surrounding multiple age groups. The large

Figure 5:
Projected Baldwin City Population Pyramid (2030)

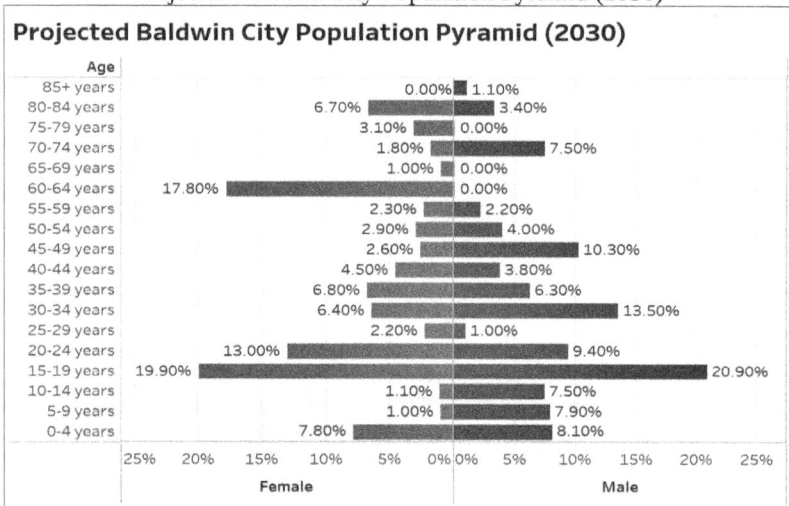

Projected Baldwin City Population Pyramid (2030)

Age	Female	Male
85+ years	0.00%	1.10%
80-84 years	6.70%	3.40%
75-79 years	3.10%	0.00%
70-74 years	1.80%	7.50%
65-69 years	1.00%	0.00%
60-64 years	17.80%	0.00%
55-59 years	2.30%	2.20%
50-54 years	2.90%	4.00%
45-49 years	2.60%	10.30%
40-44 years	4.50%	3.80%
35-39 years	6.80%	6.30%
30-34 years	6.40%	13.50%
25-29 years	2.20%	1.00%
20-24 years	13.00%	9.40%
15-19 years	19.90%	20.90%
10-14 years	1.10%	7.50%
5-9 years	1.00%	7.90%
0-4 years	7.80%	8.10%

Source: Authors Calculation (2023)

percentage of 15–24-year-olds, coupled with the severe drop off into the 25–29-year age range, is an area that needs to be addressed. Another concern is the significant variation in the 35–54-year age range considering both male and female citizens. Finally, the second highest demographic group in 2030 will be females aged 60-64; the following age groups of those 65 and older show drastic variation between genders and have overall low percentages

(US Census Bureau, 2023). Therefore, Baldwin City must create more evenly distributed age demographics based on this projected population pyramid to have a sustainable future and growth potential.

TARGETED AGE GROUPS

Teenagers and Young Adults (15-24 years old):

In Baldwin City's 2030 age demographic projections, 22% of the female and almost 30% of the male population will be between 15 and 24 years old (US Census Bureau, 2023). These high percentages result from the students attending Baldwin High School and Baker University, both in

Baldwin High School

Baldwin City. This demographic skew is understandable due to these two institutions and would be manageable if not for the severe drop-off in the following age group. Based on this data, it can be concluded that once the age of 25 is reached, most Baldwin City citizens complete any educational instruction they receive from Baldwin City High School or Baker University.

Therefore, the young people choose not to remain in Baldwin City after graduating. This is a serious issue that will need to be addressed for sustainable growth to occur.

Millennials (27-42 years old):

There is little consistency within the 27–42-year age demographic in the projections of Baldwin City's population (US Census Bureau, 2023). In a typical healthy population pyramid, this age range tends to be larger, if not the most significant percentage. Millennials are a vital part of the growth of any city. These individuals are typically more developed in their careers and financially stable. They are also more likely to be looking to start families and put down roots. Therefore, this demographic needs to be attracted to and nurtured in Baldwin City to boost the economy and rapid growth.

Older Baldwin City Neighborhood of single-family homes

Senior Citizens (65+ years old):

The 2030 demographic projections of Baldwin City show that the 60-64 age range will be the second highest. However, the drop-off is stark when looking at the following age range of 65-69, and the pattern continues to dwindle as age increases (US Census Bureau, 2023). A drop-off in senior citizens in a Midwest community is not uncommon due to the less beautiful weather. However, the jump in Baldwin City's demographic data is too severe to attribute to standard migration patterns of seniors. There needs to be an active focus on making improvements for senior citizens, as they must be recognized as an essential part of the community. A city's steps to accommodate and support its senior citizens indicate its dedication to the community's prosperity.

Senior housing duplexes

41

RECOMMENDATIONS

Reduce Brain Drain:

Brain drain, the trend of out-migration of college-educated individuals from a community, is a severe concern for Baldwin City (US Census Bureau, 2023). The drastic drop in population percentage after college-age kids indicates they are choosing to leave town and pursue a career elsewhere. To combat this brain drain, policymakers need to understand what features in a community young people value most. For example, Fiore et al. (2015) found that graduating college seniors from rural communities indicated that the cost of living and the strength of the local economy were essential factors. To ensure a reasonable cost of living for recent graduates, some changes in Baldwin City must be made.

• First, there must be more affordable housing complexes. Baldwin City currently lacks cheap apartments, and part of the strategic plan of the Baldwin City Economic Development Corporation (BCEDC) is to improve housing availability in the community (BCEDC, 2021). There needs to be a concerted effort to build new complexes where young graduates can live in a community together to enhance socialization while keeping rent costs at a reasonable rate. Without an affordable place to live, there no sense in making further adjustments to Baldwin City regarding its young people.

• After addressing the housing shortage, Baldwin City must address its lack of access to essential shopping at competitive prices. The currently available businesses to purchase critical household and grocery items are insufficient for most individuals and operate outside the budget of most recent college graduates (Sperling, 2023). The result is that most young

Apartment complex on Ninth Street

people will need to travel to surrounding areas for their necessities and therefore fail to put money back into Baldwin City's economy. Bringing bigger multinational competitive retail stores to the city will ensure affordable essentials for residents and keep their money circulating in Baldwin City's economy.

The economy's strength is the second important factor for attracting recent graduates to rural communities. Young people looking to begin their professional careers are looking to reside in a healthy economy with opportunities for economic and personal growth (Fiore et al., 2015). To ensure this is the case, policymakers need to be aware of their responsibility to ensure that economic instability is not why college graduates overlook Baldwin City. There are various ways that the local government and economic development agencies can enhance these community features that graduates seek. For example, policies that offer competitive salaries and benefits for locating a business within Baldwin City would be very influential. Also, offering more business loans and ensuring that Baldwin City fully supports entrepreneurial ventures is a great way to keep recent graduates in the town while supporting the overall economy (Fiore et al., 2015).

Eighth Street business district

Additionally, creating an environment where current college students feel connected to their surrounding town and can see a future after graduation is vital to reducing the effects of brain drain. Fiore et al. (2015) stated that "supporting partnerships between local businesses and institutions of higher education that 'fast track' skilled employees" benefits those businesses and encourages graduates to stick around. Therefore, Baldwin City officials must make more concerted efforts to connect with local companies and Baker University. In doing so, students can have more internships, shadowing, and

Entrepreneurial opportunities are important for the community.

career development opportunities in Baldwin City while still in school and form relationships that might develop into a set job opportunity upon graduation. Ensuring Baker University students are given legitimate career opportunities within Baldwin City would significantly reduce the brain drain and allow these highly educated young people to stick around to improve the community.

Baker University graduating class

Attract Millennials:

Millennials, typically known as those in the age range of 27-42 years old, are crucial for the growth of communities (Shaffner, 2021). This age demographic is typically more set in their career path and, therefore, able to contribute to a city's economic growth. This age group is also more likely to be looking to start families and settle down in a town. New residents looking to move to a rural community are greatly influenced by the quality of public schooling (Marre, 2020). Therefore, to attract and retain the millennial age demographic in Baldwin City, there needs to be a continued focus on improving K-12 education. According to Baldwin City Unified School District 348 (BCUSD – 348), Baldwin City is home to four different public schools: Baldwin Elementary School Primary Center (pre-k – 2nd grade), Baldwin Elementary School Intermediate Center (3rd – 5th grade), Baldwin Junior High School (6th – 8th grade), and Baldwin High School (9th – 12th grade).

Baldwin Elementary School Primary Center

According to Baldwin City public schools' 2022-2026 strategic plan, there are four target areas of focus for the future: preparing students for

Baldwin Elementary School Intermediate Center

Baldwin Junior High School Performing Arts Center

success, supporting the needs of students and staff, engagement in schools and school activities, and operational effectiveness (BCUSD – 348, 2023). In addition, a high standard of public schooling is critical for millennial families looking to settle in Baldwin City. Therefore, the Baldwin City school system must continue to improve and follow through on its strategic plan to ensure that families see the community as a great place to raise their children.

Additionally, childcare access goes hand-in-hand with supporting families in a city. Baldwin City currently has very few stand-alone daycare or childcare options besides the program run through the Baldwin City Recreation Commission. This program has before and after-school care for grades pre-k through 5th grade and is run primarily out of the Baldwin Elementary School Intermediate Center (Baldwin City Rec Commission, 2023). However, more childcare access is imperative to encourage millennial parents to continue pursuing their career goals and contribute to Baldwin City's economy while raising a family.

Rainbow Experience Preschool

"Yogi Bear" park on High Street

Another avenue for attracting millennials to Baldwin City is career incentives. In today's workforce, many people are taking advantage of the option to work remotely. Workers might have a fully-remote job or only go into an office a few times a week. This dramatically increases the opportunities for individuals and families who want to move to a small town but worry about the current job opportunities (Marre, 2020). Continuous broadband upgrades must be throughout the city to ensure remote working ([non]-&-millennials) can move to Baldwin City. There must be equal access to high-speed Internet across the city so that remote work at any level is an option for all ([non]-&-millennial) workers.

Other incentives that would benefit millennials in Baldwin City might be student loan repayments or tax credits for people who move to the community (Shaffner, 2021). The state of Kansas currently has a program called Kansas Rural Opportunity Zones (ROZ) which covers ninety-five counties. Moving to those counties means the new full-time resident can

Clearwave Fiber internet company

receive financial incentives such as student loan repayment assistance and a 100% state income tax credit (Kansas Department of Commerce, 2023). Unfortunately, Baldwin City is located in Douglas County, KS, which is not currently considered a Rural Opportunity Zone (ROZ) due to the high population of its neighboring city, Lawrence, KS (Kansas Department of

Commerce, 2023). However, this program has had substantial success, so Baldwin City might consider mirroring some of the opportunities and incentives the ROZ program offers on a smaller scale for those who move to the Baldwin community. These incentives can put Baldwin City on the map when millennial families seek suitable places to call home.

Businesses along High Street in downtown Baldwin City

Finally, continuing improvements to Baldwin City's downtown could go a long way in attracting millennials. In 2021, Baldwin City announced that it would be included in the Kansas City Main Street program, which gives "technical assistance in all areas of the Main Street Approach designed to further economic development downtown" as well as providing state and national grant funds (Kansas Department of Commerce, 2022). This program will help Baldwin City improve its downtown area and revitalize the community. In addition, Baldwin has made a few plans to update and refresh the town in the past three years. These renovations include their Brick Street Restoration Project to preserve the brick roads in town and the Community Center Project, which has plans to significantly update the current community center to become a "civic community space for all" (Baldwin City, 2023). Continuing to make upgrades to common town spaces and utilizing the Kansas City Main Street program to strategically increase the vibrancy of Baldwin City's downtown strategically will effectively attract millennials and young families.

The Bauer Building, slated to become a community center

Support Senior Population:

The final age demographic to focus on within Baldwin City is its senior population, age 65 and over. There is currently a spike in the 60-64 age range in Baldwin City that significantly drops off moving into the senior citizen age range (US Census Bureau, 2023). Therefore, city leaders need to understand where the disconnect may be and how to create a healthier, more viable community for senior citizens. The first issue is the lack of senior housing or senior living opportunities within Baldwin City. Researchers at the Rural Health Research Gateway studied aging in place, or the "phenomenon of people remaining in their homes and communities as they get older, even if their health status changes" (Hening-Smith & Lahr, 2022). In this study, a survey of the rural health offices in all fifty US states found that 89% of respondents felt that senior housing was a barrier to aging in place in rural areas (Hening-Smith & Lahr, 2022).

Vintage Park Retirement Center

Therefore, there is a significant need for senior-specific housing to adequately accommodate the aging of the older population in communities. Baldwin City has one senior living facility, Vintage Park, which houses about 140 seniors (Vintage Park, 2023). However, the projected range of senior citizens in Baldwin City for the next five years is between 600 and 650 residents (US Census Bureau). Therefore, Baldwin City must consider adding additional senior-specific housing or living facility to support the community's future senior citizens.

Another critical aspect of senior living in rural communities is public transportation. The Rural Health Research Gateway also found in its survey that 81% of respondents strongly agreed that transportation was a barrier to aging in rural areas (Hening-Smith & Lahr, 2022). Unfortunately, there is currently no public transportation available in Baldwin City. This creates

Baldwin City Senior Wheels

serious issues for the senior population, especially for residents who are no longer driving. Vintage Park does offer transportation to medical appointments for its residents, but seniors not residing in that assisted living facility have few options (Vintage Park, 2023.). Baldwin City needs to create public transportation, if not for all of the community, at least focused on the senior population who cannot drive themselves. This will help current seniors feel more comfortable as they continue aging within Baldwin City and let other seniors who may be weary of moving to Baldwin City know that the community will care for and support all residents at any stage.

CONCLUSION

This study aims to identify Baldwin City's population growth trends and age group distribution to provide strategic insights that will inform policymakers. Results show that Baldwin City has had an increasingly slow population growth rate over the last ten years, and its projected growth rate over the next ten years is 0.04%. Additionally, the age groups unevenly distributed within the community and threaten its growth are teenagers and young adults, millennial families, and senior citizens. Strategies to reduce the out-migration of young, college-educated people in Baldwin City include building affordable housing complexes, bringing a commercial shopping center, implementing economic policies for competitive salaries and business loans, supporting entrepreneurial ventures, and creating connections and career opportunities between local businesses and institutions of higher education. To attract millennial families, Baldwin City should continue improving its K-12 public education system and childcare access, offer career incentives to move to town, such as student loan repayment assistance or tax credit, and continue improving Baldwin City's downtown. Finally, to support the senior citizens in the community, Baldwin City should build more senior-specific housing and create a public transportation system for seniors who are no longer driving.

Baldwin City Pubic Library offering a variety of services to all ages

REFERENCES

Baldwin City Rec Commission. (2023). *Child Care*. After School Care | Baldwin City Rec Commission, KS. Retrieved 2023, from https://www.baldwinrec.org/191/After-School-Care

Baldwin City USD 348. (2023). *Baldwin City USD 348*. USD 348 Baldwin Public Schools. Retrieved 2023, from https://www.usd348.com/

Baldwin City. (2023). Baldwin City, Kansas. Retrieved 2023, from https://www.baldwincity.org/

BDEDC. (2021, January). *Goals for Baldwin City Economic Development Corp*. Baldwin City Economic Development Corporation. Retrieved 2023, from https://www.baldwincity.org/index.php?section=bc-eco-devo&cas_cscid=32&casid=213

Fiore, A. M., Niehm, L. S., Hurst, J. L., Son, J., Sadachar, A., Russell, D. W., Swenson, D., & Seeger, C. (2015). Will they stay, or will they go? Community features important in migration decisions of recent university graduates. *Economic Development Quarterly*, 29(1), 23–37. https://doi.org/10.1177/0891242414559070

Henning-Smith, C., & Lahr, M. (2022, January 18). *Aging in Place in Rural America: Challenges, opportunities, and policy initiatives*. Rural Health Research Gateway. Retrieved May 1, 2023, from https://www.ruralhealthresearch.org/webinars/aging-in-place

Kansas Department of Commerce. (2022, February 14). *Kansas Main Street*. Kansas Department of Commerce. Retrieved 2023, from https://www.kansascommerce.gov/program/community-programs/main-street/

Kansas Department of Commerce. (2023, January 6). *Rural Opportunity Zones (ROZ)*. Kansas Commerce. Retrieved 2023, from https://www.kansascommerce.gov/program/taxes-and-financing/rural-opportunity-zones-roz/4

Marre, A. (2020). Rural Population Loss and Strategies for Recovery. *Econ Focus*. Retrieved 2023, from chrome-extension://efaidnbmnnnibpcajpcglclefindmkaj/https://

www.richmondfed.org/-/media/RichmondFedOrg/publications/research/
econ_focus/2020/q1/full_issue.pdf.

Osiobe, E. (2018). A Local Economic Development Action Plan for Pennington
County, South Dakota. 10.13140/RG.2.2.11907.55846.

Osiobe E. U. & Quillen, T. (2023) *A Historical Review of Baldwin City, Kansas,
USA*. The Baker Economic Development Office [BEDO] Bulletin.

Shaffner, C. (2021, April 14). *Millennials could be a boon to smaller communities.
How can those towns attract younger workers?* Route Fifty. Retrieved 2023, from
https://www.route-fifty.com/management/2020/08/millennials-smaller-communities-
attract-younger-workers/168084/

Sperling. (2023). *Compare Cost of Living: Baldwin City, KS vs. Lecompton, KS.*
2023 compare cities' cost of living. Retrieved May 2, 2023, from
https://www.bestplaces.net/compare-cities/baldwin_city_ks/lecompton_ks/
costofliving

US Census Bureau. (2023). *Explore census data*. Explore Census Data. Retrieved
2023, from https://data.census.gov/

Vintage Park. (2023). *Home* [Facebook page]. Facebook. Retrieved 2023 from
https://www.facebook.com/vintageparkatbaldwincity/

Ejiro U. Osiobe

INDUSTRY ANALYSIS

Authors: Ejiro U. Osiobe and Henry Dobson

BALDWIN CITY, Kansas (BC—KS), is a rural town home to the oldest University in the State, a lively downtown, and a short distance from the Kansas City metropolitan area. For many, this town is a pass-through, but many miss the opportunity for growth within its borders. The issue with this is that many investors and prospective business owners do not see the use in investing time and money in a small town that is assumed to be a hub for business. This chapter will consider the industries already thriving in BC and compare them to other sectors deemed successful in other rural towns in the United States (US). This study will prove that Baldwin City is a highly prospective town due to its opportunity for growth and prosperity. In addition, the study utilizes industry data to analyze and compare the regional areas of BC—KS, Douglas County (DC), and KS. This will provide essential insights into BC's success and how the city can improve and grow (Douglas County, 2023).

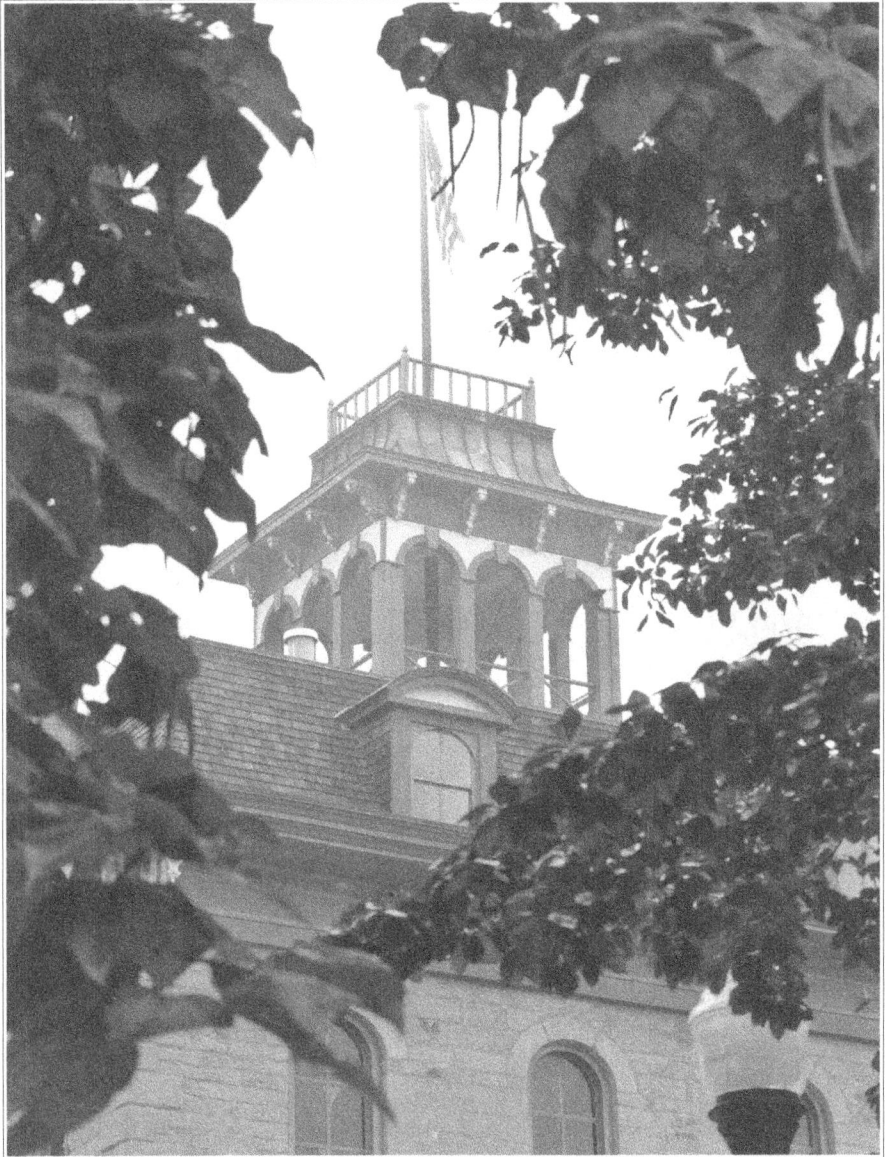

Parmenter Hall bell tower, Baker University

CHRONICLES

Albrecht (2020) researched twenty-first-century rural economies and why they are fleeting. He notes that rural economies are struggling due to enhancements in technology. Rural economies relied on goods-providing services, specifically in energy production and manufacturing. In addition, (Albrecht, 2020) hypothesized that rural communities must adapt to the new global climate since many jobs once provided for rural communities are

Baldwin State Bank, the oldest and one of three banking institutions in the city

being modernized by technology and can be done with fewer, more educated employees. Albrecht (2020) concludes that rural communities must innovate their industries, not attempt to continue the same production as before. Other scholars in the economic development field, Rupasingha et al. (2019), researched multiple governmental loans and grant-providing programs for businesses in rural areas, namely the Business and Industry Guaranteed Loan Program. Their research included success rates of these government-issued loans on the rural companies receiving them on the precedence of growth both financially and with employment. They found that businesses receiving the loans could grow at minimal rates and reduce the percentage of failure for these businesses. This research is necessary when considering remedies for failing businesses in rural areas.

INDUSTRIES ANALYSIS

Industries in Baldwin City, Kansas

While Baldwin City might seem like a small town with very little business occurring, the city has many industries at work as the city continues to grow. The largest and most booming sector in the city is education. One significant impact of this, and the city's focal point so far, is Baker University, the oldest University in the State (Baker University, 2023). The University provides jobs, high-level education, entertainment, research, and many other positive impacts on the city. While BC might be considered by many as a "college town," there are also five different schools that provide jobs and a stellar education for city residents.

Mabee Hall on Baker University campus

Like many rural communities in America, retail trade is another primary industry prevalent in BC. Retail trade is the sale of goods and services to consumers. The downtown area of BC is home to several local businesses in one location. The stores in downtown BC offer various goods

Figure 1:

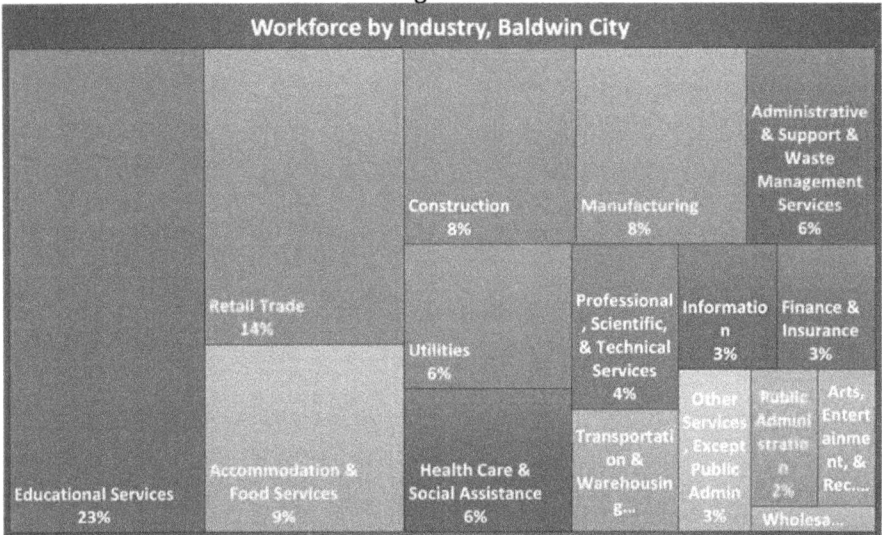

Industries in Baldwin City, Kansas (2023)

and services, from restaurants, bakeries, coffee shops, boutiques, and many more (Douglas County, 2023). These stores are mainly locally owned and run from within the borders of BC, and the town is committed to supporting small businesses. Many small businesses in similar rural cities struggle to succeed based on their consumer market, but the BC consumer market is a big supporter of local businesses. The most significant way that the town supports its local business is by hosting the Maple Leaf Festival (MLF) every year. The festival is held annually in October, bringing thousands of residents and regional tourists to spend weekends in this quaint town. But during the spring season, the city explodes with the bright colors from the trees and the streets of vendors, both local and regional. The festival is an excellent opportunity for local businesses as many different vendors and companies will set up their tents, grills, and displays to take advantage of arguably the best weekend financially for them (Douglas County, 2023).

Vendors lining Eighth Street at Maple Leaf Festival

Hundreds of vendors look to make many sales, and the entire town is involved in this great weekend. Everyone finds themselves on the brick streets of BC, from students to residents, local businesses, and traveling vendors, and many make a good profit. Elementary and middle schools offer shuttle services for a small fee, which allows the programs to make a profit for little labor. Vendors look to make high profits as some highly viewed vendors can make tens of thousands of dollars in one weekend. The economic benefits of the MLF have no ceiling as the festival continues to grow each year, bringing more money and success to BC. Also, of the retail trade sector, food retail is the most common retail industry in BC. There are multiple restaurants, from fast food to more casual dining. As for fast food, five restaurants are on the same road (N 300 Rd) (Douglas County, 2023).

El Patron, downtown Baldwin City

This main highway passes through BC, connecting Edgerton City and Olathe City. This allows commuters to see these locations and be tempted to stop, adding to the economy. There are also casual dining locations in Baldwin City. These everyday dining locations include the Wooden Spoke, El Patron, Homestead Kitchen & Bakery, and Flatlanders Pizzeria (Douglas County, 2023).

These three industries are the front-runners in BC, and any city resident will tell you that these are the primary drivers. However, with the top industries identified, it is also important to analyze some struggling industries in Baldwin. This valuable information can be vital to growing the city economically by increasing employment and popularity within more industries. Construction, manufacturing, and waste management are three industries in BC that are doing well but failing to the level that the economic developers would envision (US Census Bureau, 2023). Construction is a leading industry in any town or city around the country. Developers are

New construction replacing demolition in downtown Baldwin City

constantly looking to upgrade and expand their cities with new buildings, parks, and residential living to grow the population and economy. Unfortunately, this industry is not thriving as much in BC because BC is smaller than most cities and is often dormant in expansion. Renovations are common in the town, which keeps this construction industry moving, but much more can be done. Construction can grow depending on the near future of the city's top industries, as these industries can begin upgrades which call for more construction demand. Manufacturing is another industry that is often a critical economic growth industry in other cities. Manufacturing in BC faces similar issues to that of construction. The town is now much smaller than most towns around the country. Because of this, no major manufacturing companies see Baldwin City as a viable location for their company to grow. That said, there are still a few manufacturing companies in Baldwin City. The industry employs 169 citizens as of 2020 (Industries in BC—KS, 2023). This industry could quickly expand as the population increases. Baldwin City could even be the hub for a more prominent manufacturer if the city grows as developers envision (Douglas County, 2023).

Rice Precision Manufacturing

Waste management is the third industry that is doing well for itself but could improve. The city has found a viable routine for removing waste and keeping the city clean. The problem with this industry is that the city contracts waste management with Ottawa Sanitation Service, located in Ottawa, KS. This has worked well for BC and KS residents, but outsourcing waste management takes jobs away from residents. BC should look shortly to bring its waste management company to increase local employment and get more money into the city, not paying other towns to do the same work. While these industries are doing well in BC, some industries are struggling. These industries have not yet found their stride or have gone dormant due to outside factors. The three struggling industries are information, public administration, arts, entertainment, and recreation.

These industries are all susceptible to changing consumer preferences. BC is a small town and does not require much from the information industry. No one is searching for data insights and knowledge since the city is sometimes dormant economically. There also is no need to hire many employees in these industries. Public administration is another industry that does not need many hires in such a small town. Little administration is required for a city with just a few thousand citizens. Arts and recreation are negligible due to the population it serves. Building an arts and recreation program that succeeds in a small town with little funding is difficult. These industries are struggling in BC based on the area they serve. BC is not an excellent place for these industries to thrive, yet they survive and help the city when they can. Now that the top and bottom sectors are described for BC, it is now imperative that we compare these industries to the thriving sectors in Lawrence and the State of KS to see what works well and what does not in these local but much larger locations.

Baldwin City Recreation Commission provides activities for children and adults

Industries in Douglas County, Kansas

Figure 2:

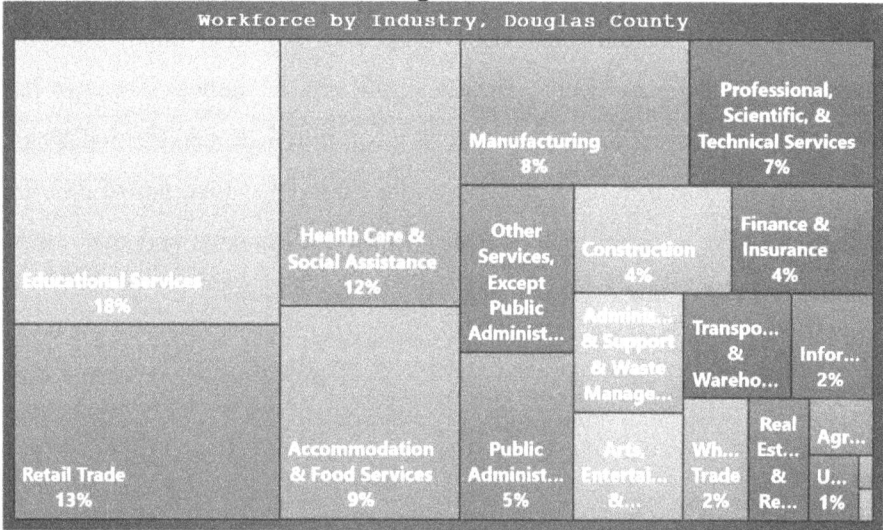

Workforce by Industry, Douglas County

Professional, Scientific, & Technical Services 7%	
Manufacturing 8%	
Health Care & Social Assistance 12%	Other Services, Except Public Administ...
Construction 4%	Finance & Insurance 4%
Educational Services 18%	Admini... & Support & Waste Manage...
Transpo... & Wareho...	Infor... 2%
Accommodation & Food Services 9%	Public Administ... 5%
Arts, Entertai... &...	Wh... Trade 2%
Real Est... & Re...	Agr... U... 1%
Retail Trade 13%	

Douglas County, KS. (2023).

DC is a relatively large county in the State of KS. The main cities within the County are Lawrence, Eudora, and BC. Lawrence is the largest in the County, with just under 100,000 residents (US Census Bureau, 2023), and home to the University of Kansas. Because of this, most of the industry's success is weighted by Lawrence. Douglas County is home to a diverse range of industries that contribute to its thriving economy. Some of the booming sectors in the County include technology, healthcare, education, arts, and culture. As the home of the University of Kansas, DC has a strong education sector providing K-12 schools, community colleges, and vocational schools. In addition, the University of Kansas is a significant employer in the area, with more than 7,000 faculty and staff members. Baker University and Haskell University also fall within Douglas County's boundaries, Baker

73

University being the oldest University in Kansas, and Haskell Indian Nations University, a highly touted tribal university (EDC Lawrence, 2019). Retail is a significant industry in DC, with major retailers such as Target, Walmart, and Best Buy in the County, found in Lawrence. The retail sector in the County provides employment opportunities to residents and serves the community's shopping needs. However, the rise of online shopping has impacted the industry, and retailers must adapt to remain competitive (Page, 2023). This has caused retail to drop to the County's second tier of thriving industries. This is comparable to every other city, County, and State as e-commerce has become a driving competitor nationwide.

Medical services in Baldwin City

The healthcare industry is another significant contributor to DC's economy, with major employers including Lawrence Memorial Hospital and Kansas University Medical Center. The city also has a strong network of medical clinics and practices, providing residents access to high-quality healthcare services. DC also has many subsidiaries of healthcare providers around the County to offer high-level healthcare to its residents. Overall, the success of these industries in DC can be attributed to the city's diverse economy, skilled workforce, and supportive business environment. As a result, these industries will likely continue to thrive, providing employment opportunities and economic growth for the Lawrence community. Middle industries in DC—KS refer to those that are neither the top-performing nor struggling industries. For example, some significant sectors in DC are retail, manufacturing, construction, and agriculture. In addition, DC is home to a growing technology sector with a per capita growth value of 19.3%, meaning the population working in technology has grown significantly in the past few years (Bascom, 2022). The University of Kansas also plays a role in this industry, with its strong computer science and engineering programs attracting talented students and researchers. Furthermore, Brian McClendon, the creator of Google Earth's "Street View," grew up in Lawrence and had ties to the city (Bascom, 2022).

Heritage Tractor supplying the farm and home community in Eastern Kansas

DC's diverse manufacturing sector includes food and beverage production, pharmaceuticals, and construction materials. The industry

Grain elevators towering over the tracks in Baldwin City

provides well-paying jobs and contributes to the County's economic growth. However, the industry faces challenges such as competition from overseas manufacturers and changes in consumer demand. The construction industry in DC has been steady in recent years, with the need for new housing and commercial properties driving growth. However, enterprises can be impacted by factors such as changes in interest rates, zoning regulations, and labor shortages. Agriculture is an essential industry in the surrounding region of DC, with farmers producing wheat, corn, and soybean crops. The sector provides food and income to the community but can be impacted by weather conditions and changes in commodity prices. DC does not have as big of an agriculture industry as other areas in the State. This is due in large part to the reduced rural land. Medium enterprises in DC face some challenges but continue to play an essential role in the County's economy. These industries provide employment opportunities and contribute to the community's economic stability. However, as the economy evolves, these industries must adapt to remain competitive and relevant in the DC market.

DC—KS has a diverse economy, but some industries have struggled recently. Some of the struggling industries in DC include printing, textile manufacturing, automotive manufacturing, and banking. The printing and publishing industry has faced significant challenges due to the rise of digital media. In DC and specifically in Lawrence, the industry has declined in recent years, with the closure of local printing businesses such as Allen Press (Lawhorn, 2023). In addition, the industry faces challenges as consumers increasingly turn to digital media for their information and entertainment needs. Lawrence also produces its newspaper, LJ World, which has increased its online presence as this is today's new preference.

DC's textile and apparel manufacturing industry has also struggled recently, with several businesses closing or relocating. The industry faces competition from overseas manufacturers and changes in consumer demand.

Twill Trade, a retail clothing outlet in downtown Baldwin City

Most demand for clothing is manufactured in major cities, not in smaller towns. DC is known for its vibrant arts and culture scene often found in Lawrence, which includes live music venues, theaters, and museums. In addition, the city hosts various events throughout the year, such as the Lawrence Arts Center's annual Art Tougeau parade, the Free State Festival, and the Busker Festival. The arts and culture sector provides the community entertainment and economic benefits, attracting tourists and creating jobs. While this is not the most employed industry due to minimal funding, DC residents emphasize this industry.

While DC has several thriving banks, the banking industry has faced challenges recently due to regulations and consumer behavior changes. For example, many consumers now rely on online banking and mobile apps, reducing the need for traditional brick-and-mortar bank branches (Shirzadi et al., 2017). Additionally, fluctuating interest rates and increased competition have impacted the industry's profitability. Overall, these struggling industries in Douglas County face various challenges, from changes in consumer behavior to competition from overseas manufacturers. However, the city's diverse economy and supportive business environment allow these industries to adapt and innovate to remain competitive. As the County continues to grow and evolve, it will be necessary for these industries to find new ways to stay relevant and thrive in the changing economy.

Industries in the State of Kansas

Figure 3:

Workforce by Industry, Kansas

			Justice, public order	Nursing Care Facilities	Banking & related activities
Agriculture 18%	Aircraft Manufacturing 14%	Health... 8%	Grocery Stores	merchan...	Amuse... &...
			Computer Systems	Outpa... care...	Arc... en... 3% / An... pr... 3%
Energy Processing 15%	Manufacturing 12%	Tourism 6%	Insurance carriers	Truck trans...	Offices of...

KS Industry Database. (2023).

KS is a midwestern state in the US with a lot of agriculture and aviation manufacturing. So naturally, the top industries in KS are agriculture from their deep farming roots, land availability, and aviation manufacturing. KS also has a prevalent natural resources industry, with frequent availability of natural resources like oil and wind. KS is known for its agricultural sector, ranking the state among the US's top wheat, corn, and cattle producers.

Agriculture contributes significantly to the State's economy, providing jobs and income to thousands of Kansans. The State's agricultural industry has also benefited from technological innovations and farming techniques, increasing farmers' efficiency and productivity. However, while the farm sector is a critical success story in KS, it is not without its struggles. Farmers in the State have faced various challenges recently, including low commodity prices, extreme weather events, and trade disputes (Kendall, 2022). KS is home to several major aviation companies, including Boeing, Spirit AeroSystems, and Textron Aviation. The aviation industry significantly contributes to the State's economy, providing high-paying jobs and generating billions of dollars in revenue annually. Wichita is known as the "Air Capital of the World" (Air Capital of the World, 2023), with a long history of aircraft manufacturing and aviation research.

McFarlane Aviation Products

KS is rich in natural resources, including oil, natural gas, and wind energy (Keller, 2022). The State's energy industry has grown recently, with companies investing in new technologies and infrastructure to support renewable energy sources such as wind power. The industry provides employment opportunities and generates revenue for the State while helping reduce reliance on fossil fuels and promote environmental sustainability. Overall, these booming industries in KS contributed to the State's economy and workforce. In addition, they have benefitted from advancements in technology, innovation, and strategic investments, positioning them for

Mid-America Bank installed solar panels on its main branch in Baldwin City in 2010.

continued growth and success in the years to come. Some middle industries in the State of KS include manufacturing, healthcare, and tourism. These industries are thriving in their rights but not as successful as those mentioned before. KS has a strong manufacturing industry, with businesses ranging from small machine shops to large factories producing everything from electronics to furniture. While manufacturing jobs have declined in some areas due to automation and outsourcing, like DC's, the industry remains an essential source of employment and revenue for many Kansans. In addition, many of these manufacturing businesses are located in rural areas, helping support local economies in these small towns.

The healthcare industry is another significant employer in KS, with hospitals, clinics, and other healthcare providers spread throughout the State. The industry has grown in recent years due to an aging population and advances in medical technology and is expected to continue to grow in the coming years. The healthcare industry provides various job opportunities, from doctors and nurses to administrative staff and support personnel. While not typically considered a "middle" industry, tourism and hospitality play an

Morningstar Care Homes: offering long-tern, memory, and adult daycare services

essential role in KS's economy. The State boasts a range of attractions, from historic sites and museums to outdoor recreation areas and entertainment venues. As a result, visitors to the State spend billions of dollars each year, supporting businesses ranging from hotels and restaurants to souvenir shops and amusement parks. These middle industries in KS provide diverse employment opportunities and contribute to the State's economy and quality of life. While they may not receive the same level of attention as the State's largest industries, they are nonetheless vital to the State's overall economic health and well-being.

For lower-performing industries in KS, banking, retail, agriculture, and natural resources have recently declined in their best industries. Like many other parts of the country, KS has recently seen a decline in traditional brick-and-mortar retail stores. The rise of online shopping has resulted in fewer in-person shopping trips, leading to store closures and job losses in the retail sector. While some retailers have been able to adapt to the changing landscape by investing in e-commerce and other strategies, others have struggled to keep up with the competition. Banking in KS is also on the decline as an industry. This can be comparable to the national industry, as banks have declined recently. This is due to the threat of online banking and fluctuating interests, and market uncertainty. As mentioned, agriculture and natural resources are two of KS' top industries. However, these industries have seen declines as well. As the State was built on the backs of farmers and the land providing abundant natural resources for Kansans to trade and develop the economy, these industries have begun to fall slightly in recent years. As Albrecht (2020) has stated, these industries and their employment is being replaced by newer, quicker technology and a more skilled workforce. This will show a decline in employment and possibly revenue for the State of KS as the world searches for more sustainable solutions. These struggling industries in KS highlight the challenges businesses face in an ever-changing economic landscape. While some sectors have been able to adapt and thrive, others have faced significant headwinds resulting in job losses and financial difficulties. As a result, the State's economic future will depend on its ability to support existing industries while investing in new growth and development opportunities.

CONCLUSION

Baldwin City has some similar industry successes and failures when compared to Douglas County, which Lawrence heavily influences. Education and healthcare are both thriving in Baldwin City and Douglas County and employ many citizens in the local area. However, there are also similar failing industries when comparing Baldwin City and Douglas County. Retail trade has declined as e-commerce has continued to take over the consumer market with its ease and competitive pricing. These factors cannot be ignored or challenged, as the future of consumer shopping will continue to be influenced by technology. BC and DC are in steady economic spaces, thriving enough to keep citizens happy and content with their locations. Still, there are ways to go about growth and sustainability. The economy of BC can grow, but it needs a push in the right direction to grow into a bigger and better city.

REFERENCES

Air Capital of the World. (2023). www.aircapitaloftheworld.com/.

Albrecht, Don E. (Aug. 3, 2020). *Building a Resilient Twenty-First Century Economy for Rural America*. Utah State University Press. http://www.jstor.org/stable/j.ctv12sdzdz.

Baker University - Profile, Rankings, and Data | US News Best Colleges. (2023). US News. https://www.usnews.com/best-colleges/baker-university-1903.

Baker University. (18 Mar. 2023). https://www.bakeru.edu/.

Bascom, Emma. (9 Mar. 2022) *Lawrence Listed as Fast-Growing Tech Hub in Recent Study; That Could Snowball, Industry Leader Says*. The Lawrence Times. lawrencekstimes.com/2022/03/09/Lawrence-fast-growing-tech-hub/.

Douglas County, KS. (2023). Data USA. https://datausa.io/profile/geo/douglas-county-ks.

Industries in Baldwin City, Kansas (City). (2023). The Demographic Statistical Atlas of the United States - Statistical Atlas. https://statisticalatlas.com/place/Kansas/Baldwin-City/Industries.

Kansas. (2023). *Data USA*. https://datausa.io/profile/geo/kansas.

Keller, Cory. (6 Dec. 2022) *Energy & Natural Resources*. Kansas Department of Commerce. www.kansascommerce.gov/industry/energy-natural-resources/.

Kendall, Dave. (3 Apr. 2022). *History of Challenges Adds to Current Stresses for Kansas Farmers and Their Communities*. Kansas Reflector. kansasreflector.com/2022/04/03/history-of-challenges-adds-to-current-stresses-for-kansas-farmers-and-their-communities/.

Lawhorn, Chad. (23 Mar. 2023). *Signs That New Owner of Allen Press Is Cutting Jobs from Lawrence Plant*. LJ World.

Page, Lucy. (2023) *The Effect of E-Commerce Expansion on Local Retail*. NBER. www.nber.org/digest/202208/effect-e-commerce-expansion-local-retail#:~:text=E %2Dcommerce%20has%20dramatically%20altered,to%2013.3%20percent%20in %202021.

Rupasingha, A., Crown, D., & Pender, J. (2019). Rural business programs and business performance: The impact of the USDA's Business and Industry (B&I) Guaranteed Loan Program. Journal of Regional Science, 59(4), 701–722. https://doi-org.bakeru.idm.oclc.org/10.1111/jors.12421

Schools & Higher Education. (15 Mar. 2019). EDC Lawrence. edclawrence.com/living-here/schools-higher-education.

Shirzadi, Shahryar, et al. (June 2017). *Managing Small and Medium Scale Enterprises in a. - IOSR Journals*. IOSR Journal of Business and Manage-ment. iosrjournals.org/iosr-jbm/papers/Vol19-issue6/Version-1/D1906012131.pdf.

US Census Bureau Quick facts: Lawrence City, Kansas (2023). United States Census Bureau. www.census.gov/quickfacts/lawrencecitykansas.

USD 348. (2023). USD 348 Baldwin Public Schools. www.usd348.com/.

Ejiro U. Osiobe

BUSINESS ATTRACTION

Authors: Ejiro U. Osiobe and Mercedes Ruiz

This chapter uses a quantitative approach, Location Quotient (LQ), to analyze various employment industries concerning Baldwin City, Kansas, from 2013-2020. The findings of this study suggest that the LQ is a good tool for identifying Baldwin City's strengths, weaknesses, opportunities, and threats. Baldwin City is a small, rural city in Douglas County, Kansas. As of the 2020 census, Baldwin City has about 4,900 people and covers 2.7 square miles (Census Reporter, 2023).

Baldwin's history is tied to the constant migration along the Santa Fe Trail, and it has now remained a historic city emphasizing historic charm (Baldwin City, Kansas: Baldwin City Government (BCK – BCG), 2023). In addition, Baldwin City is home to Baker University, a private liberal arts college. Baker University was the first four-year university in Kansas, playing into Baldwin's historic charm (BCK – BCG, 2023).

Figure 1:

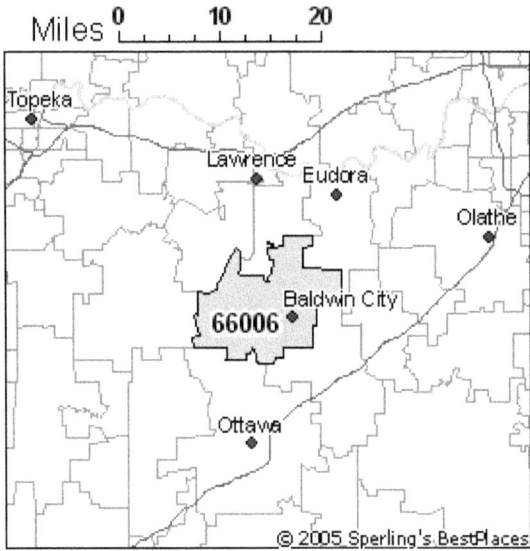

(Best Places to Live in Baldwin City
(Zip 66006), Kansas, 2023)

Baker University campus

Along with the historic charm, Baldwin has a significant community spirit and annually hosts the Maple Leaf Festival, attracting thousands of visitors annually (Maple Leaf Festival, 2023). Regarding the local economy, Baldwin City is primarily driven by educational services, construction, information, and retail trade (Baldwin City, KS | Data USA, 2023 and Douglas County | Data USA, 2023). Baldwin City offers a relaxed and friendly environment with strong historical ties and a sense of community (BCK – BCG, 2023). Figure 1 shows Baldwin City's geographical location and its neighboring cities.

CHRONICLES

Osiobe, 2018 showed that the LQ is useful for demographic analysis because it highlights the area's uniqueness. LQ analysis effectively identified industries bringing money into the region and endangered sectors of the economy that could erode the region's economic base (Osiobe, 2018). In addition, the LQ is useful in employment analysis because it illuminates what makes the region's employment unique compared to the county, state, and nation. This study defines basic status as industries that create new incomes and additional spending power in an economy. In contrast, nonbasic industries provide support services to the basic sectors (Osiobe, 2018).

Another study (Leigh,1970) emphasized that the LQ is one of the various shortcut procedures for identifying basic economic activities and estimating basic employment. Basic economic activities produce goods and services surplus to local demands and export the services to external marketing while channeling income into the local economy. Basic employment falls within industries where their LQs are one or greater (Leigh,1970).

However, (Leigh,1970) also explains some of the LQ's limitations. More specifically, the researcher found that higher LQs are identified correctly, but industries with low to medium LQs, don't identify basic and nonbasic status. Given this finding, we must be suspicious of the meaning of the LQ methodology (Leigh, 1970). Generally, the LQ is a valuable, affordable tool for economic development in regions seeking to attract businesses. The LQ analysis can help identify vital industries that provide a competitive advantage in an area, help to inform financial, economic, and community strategies, and identify gaps in a local economy that new businesses can fill. Although the LQ has limitations, it can still present material findings combined with other economic analysis tools.

EMPIRICAL MODEL

The LQ Methodology:

To further develop our understanding of Baldwin City's industrial position, the analytical tool being used will be the LQ. Given the nature of the empirical research, policymakers and economic development practitioners can base their decisions on reliable data that will foster the growth of Baldwin City and similar rural communities.

LQ – (How to find opportunity and strength of Baldwin City):

The LQ is an economic development analytical tool that shows how concentrated an industry, cluster, occupation, or demographic is in a region compared to the county, state, [and/or] nation. It identifies basic and nonbasic industries. Basic industries create new incomes and additional spending power in an economy, while nonbasic industries provide support services to the basic industries. These industries can be distinguished through the value of the LQ.

For instance, an LQ of 1.00 in Public Administration means that the region and the respected area are equally specialized in Public Administration. In contrast, an LQ of 1.2 means the region has a higher concentration in Public Administration than the respected area. In hindsight, the LQ is a ratio that compares a region to a larger reference region. For this study, our equations are as follows:

$$\frac{City}{County} \rightarrow \frac{City}{State} \rightarrow \frac{City}{Nation} = \frac{Baldwin\ City}{Douglas\ County} \rightarrow \frac{Baldwin\ City}{Kansas} \rightarrow \frac{Baldwin\ City}{United\ States}$$

Lq_i	LQ_i Interpretation
Greater than (>1)	Basic Sector/employer
Equal to (=1)	Employment is similar to the broader economy
Less than (<1)	Nonbasic Sector/employer

$$LQ_i = \left(\frac{e_i}{e}\right) \Big/ \left(\frac{A_i}{A}\right)$$

Where:

e_i = Local employment in a specific industry
e = Total local employment in all industries
A_i = County employment in a specific industry
A = Total County employment in all industries

$$LQ_i = \left(\frac{e_i}{e}\right) \Big/ \left(\frac{B_i}{B}\right)$$

Where:

e_i = Local employment in a specific industry
e = Total local employment in all industries
B_i = State employment in a specific industry
B = Total State employment in all industries

$$LQ_i = \left(\frac{e_i}{e}\right) \Big/ \left(\frac{E_i}{E}\right)$$

Where:

e_i = Local employment in a specific industry
e = Total local employment in all industries
E_i = National employment in a specific industry
E = Total National employment in all industries

Table 1 compares the figures and percentage of employment by sectors using 2019 datasets in Baldwin City, Douglas County, Kansas, and the United States (US).

Table 2 shows the LQ of Baldwin City in comparison to Douglas County, Kansas. The highlighted cells represent the basic industries. The following sectors maintained their basic status from 2013-2020, construction, educational services, information, and retail trade.

Table 3 shows the LQ of Baldwin City in comparison to Kansas. The consistent basic industries are Arts, Entertainment & Recreation and Accommodation & Food Services; Construction; Educational services, Health Care & Social Assistance; and Retail Trade. The emergence of Arts, Entertainment & Recreation, and Accommodation & Food Services as a basic industry is due to the NAICS. Industries are labeled with five-digit codes at the city and county levels, whereas at state and national levels, four-digit codes are used. In addition, the industries are often grouped and less specific at the state and federal levels.

Table 4 shows the LQ of Baldwin City compared to the US. The consistent basic industries are Arts, Entertainment & Recreation and

Accommodation & Food Services; Construction; Educational services, Health Care & Social Assistance; and Retail Trade.

Table 1:

A Comparison of the Actual Figures & Percentage of Employment by Sectors (2019) Baldwin City, Douglas County, Kansas, and the US

Industry	Baldwin City		Douglas County		Kansas		USA	
	#	%	#	%	#	%	#	%
Active Duty Military	5	0%	679	1%	17124	1%	1073229	1%
Agriculture, Forestry, Fishing and Hunting, and Mining					31569	2%	2333677	2%
Arts, Entertainment & Recreation and Accommodation & Food Services	215	10%	8276	12%	116524	8%	14491055	10%
Construction	194	9%	2832	4%	81600	6%	8846904	6%
Educational Services, Health Care & Social Assistance	599	27%	20507	30%	344192	25%	34844153	24%
Finance & Insurance, and Real Estate, Rental & Leasing	42	2%	3748	6%	82661	6%	9567195	6%
Information	51	2%	1422	2%	26152	2%	2972145	2%
Manufacturing	210	10%	5501	8%	177752	13%	15425247	10%
Other Services, Except Public Administration	39	2%	3129	5%	52168	4%	6163767	4%
Professional, Scientific & Management, and Administrative & Waste Management Services	226	10%	6626	10%	125951	9%	16191212	11%
Public Administration	58	3%	3108	5%	65472	5%	7081261	5%
Retail Trade	389	18%	8565	13%	148216	11%	16716798	11%
Transportation & Warehousing, and Utilities	147	7%	2414	4%	69300	5%	7865149	5%
Wholesale Trade	19	1%	1308	2%	40004	3%	3895587	3%
Total employment	2194		68115		1378685		147467379	

Source: Author's calculations based on the infromation from Data USA

96

Table 2:

Location Quotient of Baldwin City (Douglas County Base) for 2013-2020

Industry	2013	2014	2015	2016	2017	2018	2019	2020
Accommodation & Food Services	1.02	0.94	1.04	1.09	0.89	0.90	0.76	0.92
Administrative & Support & Waste Management Services	0.43	0.15	0.50	0.82	0.94	0.72	1.57	1.45
Agriculture, Forestry, Fishing & Hunting	0.94	0.89	0.96	0.24	0.33	0.27	0.24	0.00
Arts, Entertainment, & Recreation	0.33	1.37	1.26	1.83	1.44	1.53	0.74	0.52
Construction	2.67	3.05	3.33	2.31	2.14	2.14	1.98	1.54
Educational Services	1.14	1.24	1.27	1.06	1.38	1.33	1.09	1.12
Finance & Insurance	0.27	0.16	0.33	0.24	0.44	0.47	0.45	0.68
Health Care & Social Assistance	0.90	1.12	0.99	0.82	0.63	0.66	0.45	0.43
Information	2.39	2.09	2.14	1.52	0.81	1.21	1.04	1.41
Management of Companies & Enterprises	0.00	0.00	0.00	0.00	0.00	0.00	0.00	0.00
Manufacturing	1.25	0.68	0.73	0.86	0.92	0.88	1.10	0.89
Mining, Quarrying, & Oil & Gas Extraction	0.00	0.00	0.00	0.00	0.00	0.00	0.00	0.00
Other Services, Except Public Administration	1.61	1.66	1.49	1.22	0.68	0.68	0.36	0.51
Professional, Scientific, & Technical Services	0.81	0.85	0.74	0.52	0.85	0.73	0.70	0.54
Public Administration	0.59	0.69	0.87	0.82	1.00	0.91	0.54	0.49
Real Estate & Rental & Leasing	0.00	0.00	0.00	0.00	0.07	0.02	0.07	0.07
Retail Trade	0.87	0.73	1.06	1.00	1.09	1.07	1.31	1.05
Transportation & Warehousing	1.44	1.40	1.21	1.31	0.28	0.31	1.01	0.87
Utilities	0.00	0.00	0.00	0.00	0.66	1.40	4.32	6.03
Wholesale Trade	2.53	1.83	0.37	0.67	0.41	0.42	0.42	0.38

(Baldwin City, KS | Data USA, 2023 and Douglas County | Data USA, 2023)

Table 3:

Location Quotient for Baldwin City (Kansas Base) for 2014-2020

Industry	2014	2015	2016	2017	2018	2019	2020
Active Duty Military	0.00	0.00	0.00	0.00	0.00	0.00	0.00
Agriculture, Forestry, Fishing and Hunting, and Mining	0.28	0.33	0.07	0.09	0.09	0.10	0.00
Arts, Entertainment & Recreation and Accommodation & Food Services	1.44	1.57	1.69	1.41	1.49	1.13	1.21
Construction	2.39	2.50	1.71	1.51	1.54	1.46	1.28
Educational Services, Health Care & Social Assistance	1.51	1.45	1.21	1.39	1.35	1.07	1.06
Finance & Insurance, and Real Estate, Rental & Leasing	0.10	0.22	0.16	0.31	0.31	0.31	0.47
Information	2.71	2.75	2.05	0.99	1.36	1.20	1.54
Manufacturing	0.36	0.37	0.46	0.49	0.53	0.72	0.56
Other Services, Except Public Administration	1.91	1.58	1.39	0.79	0.85	0.46	0.69
Professional, Scientific & Management, and Administrative & Waste Management Services	0.64	0.77	0.70	0.99	0.84	1.10	1.05
Public Administration	0.52	0.72	0.79	0.97	0.88	0.54	0.43
Retail Trade	0.77	1.12	1.13	1.27	1.32	1.61	1.25
Transportation & Warehousing, and Utilities	0.60	0.55	0.67	0.23	0.40	1.30	1.61
Wholesale Trade	1.20	0.25	0.43	0.25	0.30	0.29	0.26

(Baldwin City, KS | Data USA and Kansas | Data USA, 2023)

Table 4:

Location Quotient of Baldwin City (US Base) for 2014-2020

Industry	2014	2015	2016	2017	2018	2019	2020
Active Duty Military	0.00	0.00	0.00	0.00	0.00	0.00	0.00
Agriculture, Forestry, Fishing and Hunting, and Mining	0.41	0.48	0.11	0.13	0.14	0.14	0.00
Arts, Entertainment & Recreation and Accommodation & Food Services	1.22	1.31	1.45	1.19	1.25	0.96	1.03
Construction	2.49	2.56	1.77	1.51	1.52	1.42	1.20
Educational Services, Health Care & Social Assistance	1.66	1.58	1.29	1.47	1.42	1.11	1.10
Finance & Insurance, and Real Estate, Rental & Leasing	0.09	0.20	0.14	0.28	0.28	0.28	0.43
Information	2.95	2.93	2.14	0.96	1.26	1.11	1.38
Manufacturing	0.44	0.45	0.56	0.59	0.64	0.88	0.70
Other Services, Except Public Administration	1.82	1.49	1.29	0.71	0.75	0.41	0.62
Professional, Scientific & Management, and Administrative & Waste Management Services	0.53	0.63	0.60	0.84	0.70	0.90	0.84
Public Administration	0.51	0.70	0.76	0.94	0.86	0.53	0.41
Retail Trade	0.75	1.09	1.07	1.19	1.23	1.50	1.15
Transportation & Warehousing, and Utilities	0.62	0.55	0.65	0.22	0.37	1.21	1.48
Wholesale Trade	1.26	0.27	0.47	0.26	0.33	0.31	0.27

(Baldwin City, KS | Data USA, 2023) (United States | Data USA, 2023)

The SWOT Analysis of Baldwin City in Comparison to Douglas County Based on the Five-digit NAICS Codes:

Strengths:	Weaknesses:
• Construction • Educational Services • Information • Retail Trade	• Agriculture, Forestry, Fishing & Hunting • Finance & Insurance • Management of Companies & Enterprises • Real Estate & Rental & Leasing • Mining, Quarrying, & Oil & Gas Extraction • Professional, Scientific, & Technical Services
Opportunities:	Threats:
• Utilities • Manufacturing • Transportation & Warehousing	• Wholesale • Other Services, Except Public Administration • Arts, Entertainment, & Recreation

Source: (Baldwin City, KS | Data USA, 2023)
(Douglas County | Data USA, 2023)

Strengths

The LQ has consistently identified Baldwin City's strengths compared to Douglas County, Kansas, and the US. The industries that are categorized as strengths are industries that have remained basic from 2013-2022.

Weaknesses

The LQ identified several industries as weak within Baldwin's economy. These industries are labeled vulnerable due to their nonbasic status from 2013-2020.

Opportunities

The LQ identified three industries, Utilities; Manufacturing; Transportation & Warehousing, as opportunities considering their current basic status. With these industries comes an opportunity for new businesses to solidify these industries' basic status in the upcoming years.

Threats

The LQ identified three industries, Wholesale; Other Services Except, Public Administration; Arts, Entertainment, & Recreation, as threats to their recent status change from basic to nonbasic industries. However, these industries can be nurtured back to their original basic status with support and new initiatives.

Arts and Crafts sale at the Lumberyard Arts Center

RECOMMENDATIONS

These recommendations are based on the opportunities and threats of Baldwin City, with some guidance on the city's strengths.

Subsidized Housing

Subsidized Housing doesn't necessarily mean rent control but instead building new homes, playing off our construction strength. These homes can be a place for housing for low and moderate-income earners in Kansas City, Kansas, Kansas City, Missouri, and Lawrence City. This opportunity can attract people to live in Baldwin instead of our neighboring towns. In this sense, we can make Baldwin City a sought-out destination for better living at a lower price. We'd gain more residents, attracting more business establishments to satisfy the need of the growing community.

Apartment complexes in Baldwin City

Infrastructure

In terms of infrastructure, it can work in conjunction with the subsidized housing recommendation. Renewable power through windmills can be an opportunity to create sustainable energy in Baldwin City through windmill farms. Given the drive to increase the population, local energy can help support the need for more power. In addition, public storage is a great way to maintain people's homes. One aspect of bringing more residents is curb appeal; with public storage, we'd provide places to store things and keep their yards clean of unnecessary clutter. Along with curb appeal, maintaining and creating new sidewalks is a great way to promote connectivity and community. Bike lanes improve the safety of sidewalks and increase Baldwin's population through subsidized housing; more people may work in Baldwin and could easily bike to their place of work.

Primarily, my recommendations are based on the LQs and are applied to facilitate migration to Baldwin City, but also have money spent within Baldwin City rather than neighboring cities.

CONCLUSION

Baldwin City's strengths, opportunities, weaknesses, and threats based on the LQs are helpful information for the prospective future of Baldwin City. Subsidized housing and infrastructure investment can bring and support the push for increased population, thus attracting businesses to satisfy the growing community's needs. Again, the LQ was used to analyze the various employment industries within Baldwin City. In turn, the LQ revealed the economy's most vital sectors: Construction, Educational Services, Information, and Retail Trade. These four industries are stimulating the economic flow of Baldwin. Alternatively, the LQ illuminated sectors with great potential in Baldwin, such as Utilities, Manufacturing, and Transportation & Warehousing. This paper provides insightful information to stimulate economic growth and development in Baldwin City, Kansas, and similar rural communities. The information in this document can be used by students, economic development partitioners, government officials, and policymakers.

Newly remodeled insurance and financial offices

REFERENCES

Baldwin City, Kansas: Baldwin City Government. (2023).
https://www.baldwincity.gov/community/library/index.php?section=city-govt

Baldwin City, KS | Data USA. (2023). Data USA.
 ttps://datausa.io/profile/geo/baldwin-city-ks

Best Places to Live in Baldwin City (zip 66006), Kansas. (n.d.). Best Places.
Retrieved May 1, 2023, from
https://www.bestplaces.net/zip-code/kansas/baldwin_city/66006

Census Reporter. (2023). Census profile: Baldwin City, KS.
https://censusreporter.org/profiles/16000US2003900-baldwin-city-ks/

Douglas County, KS | Data USA. (2023). Data USA.
https://datausa.io/profile/geo/douglas-county-ks

Kansas | Data USA. (2023). Data USA. https://datausa.io/profile/geo/kansas

Leigh, R. A. (1970). The Use of Location Quotients in Urban Economic Base
Studies. *Land Economics*, 46(2), 202. https://doi.org/10.2307/3145181

Maple Leaf Festival. (2023). Maple Leaf Festival. https://mapleleaffestival.com/

Osiobe, E. U. (2018). A Local Economic Development Action Plan for Pennington
County, South Dakota. *ResearchGate*. https://doi.org/10.13140/RG.2.2.11907.55846

United States | Data USA. (2023). Data USA.
https://datausa.io/profile/geo/united-states

Ejiro U. Osiobe

BUSINESS RETENTION

Authors: Ejiro U. Osiobe and Parker Straight

Implementing a business retention and expansion (BR&E) plan for Baldwin City, Kansas, will have several benefits. First, it will help businesses grow and become more committed to the community. This growth will provide more quality jobs and employment opportunities for those in Baldwin City, possibly increasing the future population. It will also allow the existing competition to remain healthy rather than pushing out fellow competitors and decreasing community business activities.

Implementing this plan will strengthen companies as they will have the needed support and help to thrive. Lastly, Baldwin City's economy will benefit from the retention and expansion as more capital is circulated through the city rather than to neighboring ones such as Lawrence. (Walker & Hall, 2023)

BR&E plans have also been very successful, as studies have shown their effectiveness. Specifically, 72% of those implementing these plans find it very beneficial. When sending out a survey to states such as Missouri and Nebraska, they were asked to detail what strategies they were implementing. Most were dealing with manufacturing, while others involved retail services and tourism. According to these plans put into place, a total of 30% had been wholly executed, while another 35% were in the process. Even if the procedure wasn't completed or in the process, 24% of the plans began. This chapter shows that when a BR&E plan is put into place, it is more likely to be carried out and achieved (Morse, 1997).

A monthly event through the summer bringing together local entrepreneurs

CHRONICLES

For this research on BR&E for Baldwin City, Kansas, we evaluate how the community can grow and incorporate shift-share analysis to determine which industries require more attention than others. Some concepts considered throughout this research include the five modules analysis, breakdown of shift-share analysis, and assessing how successful BR&E programs are.

According to (Morse, 1997), an economics professor at the University of Minnesota, BR&E programs can be very successful. Morse and his then Ph.D. student, Dr. Inhyuck, determined how BR&E programs were successful and where they were not. This study focused on BR&E programs at a state level and how much they impacted the communities within the state.

Furthermore, an analysis of BR&E done by Purdue University's economic development team evaluates how beneficial incorporating a BR&E program for a community is. This is like Morse's research, as it determines the impacts it can have on businesses and the community. Purdue involved five different modules allowing economic development teams to follow, to be precise, with their retention and expansion of companies.

Having a guideline to follow will enable BR&E programs to be particular in their work and ensures all areas are evaluated for business growth and retention in a community. Finally, these five modules' and the shift-share analysis, precisely the regional competitiveness effect, can be involved in understanding how a specific industry is doing within the community.

According to (Osiobe, 2018), an assistant professor of data analytics at Baker University, the regional competitiveness effect can determine if a particular industry is underperforming or outperforming compared to national trends. Determining the regional competitiveness effect for a specific sector will allow a community to decide which initiatives to focus on. Overall, the research found within this case study shows how beneficial

Baldwin City's historic downtown district

implementing a BR&E program for Baldwin City, Kansas, can be. Using the five modules from Purdue University and incorporating regional competitiveness effect findings will positively impact BR&E in Baldwin City, Kansas.

BUSINESS RETENTION & EXPANSION – FIVE MODULES

For the BR&E plan to be performed and executed with successful individuals, the following five modules are: Organize, Gain Support, Gather Information, Analyze Results, and Report Findings (Walker & Hall, 2023).

Organize:

To begin the BR&E plan, we must organize a group of individuals that are ready and willing to implement this program. This will include members of the city as well as business owners that are interested in taking steps forwards to improve. With the organization of a group, meetings will be held to discuss the current issues and which to tackle. These meetings are just the base, as the further steps will cover much more information (Walker& Hall, 2023).

Gain Support:

Once a group has been formed for a BR&E plan, they must also gain support from the community. Community members should also be interested and ready to help as it will be beneficial not only for the businesses but also themselves. To get the news out about the BR&E program, the groups in charge should take full advantage of media outlets. Whether through a newspaper or a social media app such as Facebook, Twitter, or Instagram, this will allow more individuals to be aware of what is happening. In addition, once they know the plans, these outlets will allow better communication between the city and its community to discover problems and find the best solutions (Walker & Hall, 2023).

Baldwin City Community Newspaper, a weekly subscription

Gathering Information:

With businesses and the community fully willing to move forward with the BR&E program, it is time to gather information about the city. A questionnaire should be sent to businesses regarding how they are currently doing, whether they have experienced any growth or decline, their current issues, and if they will be facing any in the future. Of course, there will be many other questions to understand better how the business is doing. Surveys will also be sent out to community members to understand their most significant issues and what they would like to see improvement on within the community. These surveys could also be specific and only based on a particular sector of businesses if needed (Walker & Hall, 2023).

Analyze Results:

When all questionnaires and surveys are collected, they must be thoroughly analyzed by the group members of the BR&E program. All qualitative or quantitative results will be crucial and beneficial for the business and its growth. By examining this information, the group of the BR&E program, along with the company itself, will then be able to identify the current issues and their success. With these issues, they will then be able to develop strategies to resolve them. On the other hand, taking advantage of what has already been successful in that business and using those successes to grow even further (Walker & Hall, 2023).

Report Findings:

Lastly, after analyzing and communicating with business owners about the steps for the BR&E program, it will report to the community. This will allow them to know which plans will be undergoing either currently or in the future. This will again be done through media outlets, letting more community members know the goals. Some information may be withheld from the public as it is personal, and the business is unwilling to share it (Walker & Hall, 2023).

SHIFT-SHARE ANALYSIS

A shift-share analysis will be very beneficial to understand better how business sectors are doing in Baldwin City, Kansas. Shift share analysis allows us to determine which sectors are economically growing or declining. Some of the variables used in this analysis include the amount of employment in a specific industry, employment in the first year and most recent year, and the overall change based on national trends relating to the particular sector being evaluated. The following equation is used for shift-share analysis (Osiobe, 2018).

$$\Delta e_\iota = e_{\iota,t} - e_{\iota,t-1} = NS_\iota + IM_\iota + RS_\iota \quad (1)$$

Where:

Δe_ι : Change in employment in a specific industry
$e_{\iota,t}$: Industry employment in the most recent year
$e_{\iota,t-1}$: Industry employment in the first year
NS_ι : Change due to national trends
IM_ι : Change due to industrial mix
RS_ι : Change due to regional shift

There are three changes in shift-share analysis: the national growth effect, the industry mix effect, and the regional competitiveness effect. The national growth effect is based on how the economy is doing nationally. For instance, if the national economy were declining, the industry would most likely decline. The industry mix effect looks at how much a region's growth is based on an industry's national growth. Finally, we will focus on the Regional competitiveness effect for this Baldwin City, Kansas, case study (Osiobe, 2018).

REGIONAL COMPETITIVENESS EFFECT

The regional competitiveness effect recognizes the change due to unique competitive advantage within a specific region. This equation shows employment within a particular sector in the most recent and first years. We also look at national employment for the same industry to compare how the Baldwin City, Kansas, sector is based on national employment. (Osiobe, 2018).

$$\mathbf{R}si = ei{,}t\text{-}1 * \left(\frac{ei{,}t - ei{,}t\text{-}1 - Ei{,}t - Ei{,}t\text{-}1}{ei{,}t\text{-}1 \qquad Ei{,}t\text{-}1} \right) \qquad (2)$$

Where:

$\mathbf{R}si$: Change due to regional shift
ei,t: Regional employment in industry in the most recent year
$ei,t\text{-}1$: Regional employment in industry in the first year
$\mathbf{E}i,t$: National employment in industry in the most recent year
$\mathbf{E}i,t\text{-}1$: National employment in industry in the first year
(Osiobe, 2018).

The two major sectors we will evaluate using the regional competitiveness effect for Baldwin City, Kansas, are educational services and retail trade. The regional competitive effect can be used to determine other industries in Baldwin City and how they are doing compared to national trends. For instance, if a certain industry has a negative regional effect, then the Baldwin Economic Development can focus on improving that industry specifically. On the other hand, if an industry has a positive regional effect, it can figure out why they are thriving and continue to expand using the methods that bring that industry up.

EDUCATIONAL SERVICES

Baldwin City's most prominent industry for many years has been educational services which, according to the 2020 census data, has 480 individuals employed (Baldwin City, KS, 2020). From 2015 to 2020, employment had dropped by 61 people while national employment increased by 70,591. Although employment within the education services has fallen, possibly due to outside factors such as Covid—19, the industry is outperforming national trends for Baldwin City. This can be seen as the

Table 1:
Regional Competitiveness Effect of Educational
Services in Baldwin City, KS

Year	Employed	National Employment	Regional Effect
2015	541	12,367,360	1.572
2016	455	12,537,374	-93.437
2017	599	12,721,094	137.333
2018	585	12,941,888	-24.397
2019	475	13,058,235	-115.259
2020	480	12,437,951	27.563

Source:
Employed – (Baldwin City, KS. 2020)
National Employment – (Le, 2023)
Regional Effect - (Authors' Calculation, 2023)

regional competitiveness effect was positive in 2020 as well as in 2015 and 2017. However, in 2016, 2018, and 2019 Baldwin City's educational services were underperforming compared to national trends (See Table 1). This can be seen as the regional effect was negative within those years. Overall, the regional competitiveness effect fluctuates greatly for the educational services industry for Baldwin City as it is currently underperforming.

RETAIL TRADE

Retail trade is another primary industry in Baldwin City, with 295 individuals employed, according to 2020 census data (Baldwin City, KS, 2020). From 2015 to 2020, employment has increased by 22, showing that the industry is growing. However, compared to national trends in 2020 and

Table 2:
Regional Competitiveness Effect of Retail
Trade in Baldwin City, KS

Year	Employed	National Employment	Regional Effect
2015	273	17689631	83.175
2016	273	17971516	-4.350
2017	306	17799141	35.618
2018	317	17786546	11.217
2019	389	17793309	71.879
2020	295	17930357	-96.996

Source:
Employed – (Baldwin City, KS. 2020)
National Employment – (Thomas, 2023)
Regional Effect - (Authors' Calculation, 2023)

2016, retail trade for Baldwin City was underperforming due to a negative regional competitiveness effect. Every other year including 2015, 2017, 2018, and 2019 the retail trade industry for Baldwin City outperformed the national trend with a positive regional competitive effect. Overall, retail trade for Baldwin City, Kansas, has been doing good compared to national trends rather than most recently, where in 2020, it dropped down drastically.

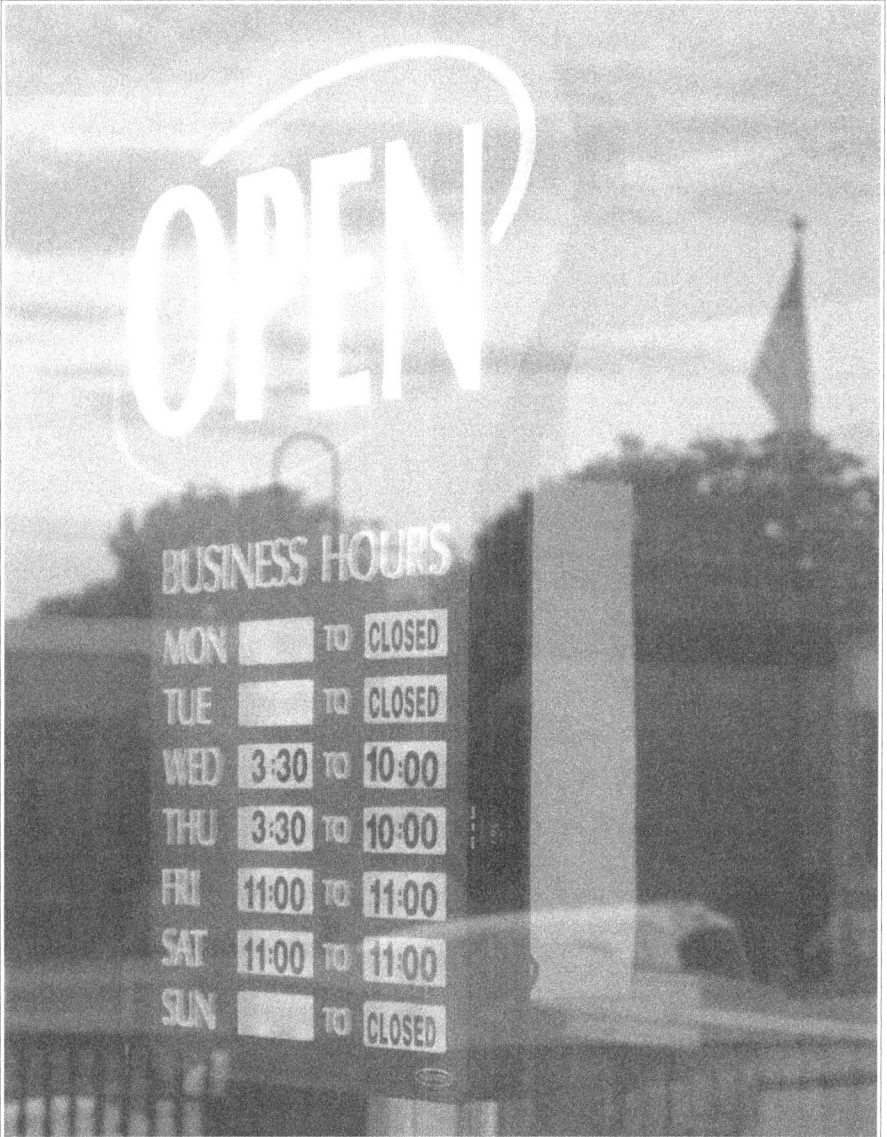

ECONOMIC DEVELOPMENT PLANS/GOALS

Baldwin City, Kansas, had created an economic development plan in 2021 that recognized their 1-year goals, 3-year goals, as well as 10-year goals. The 1-year goals included weekly advertising, averaging around 500 dollars a month, and promoting Baker University. Considering Baker University is Baldwin City's most significant employer, promoting the university would connect the students with the community and support them. The 3-year goals involved creating 15 jobs and more affordable housing, especially for senior citizens. Lastly, with 10-year plans, they would like to develop a park and have business revolving loan funds with 300,000 dollars towards assisting business expansion (Goals for Baldwin City Economic Development Corp., 2021).

RECOMMENDATIONS

With the Baldwin City economic development team's current goals, some recommendations can be made to improve these goals. For example, in the one-year plan, Baldwin City would like to promote Baker University as it is a significant part of this city. However, instead of just promoting the university, it is recommended to partner with them. Partnering with Baker University would allow the city to access classes such as business analytics, data projects, and other major business classes that could be utilized in helping the economic development of Baldwin City, Kansas. Additionally, with 3-year goals, they wanted to create more jobs. However, they weren't specific as to what type. It is recommended that they focus on particular industry jobs that are possibly dissipating or declining. This would allow those businesses that are struggling to be assisted.

CONCLUSION

In conclusion, implementing a BR&E plan for Baldwin City, Kansas, will significantly impact the growth and expansion of businesses within the community. It will allow the economic development team to reach attainable goals while supporting firms and their specific needs. The five modules will give them a complete analysis of particular industries and their current situations. Also, utilizing shift-share analysis, precisely the regional competitiveness effect, to determine which industries are increasing or declining compared to national trends. This will give the economic development team enough information to recognize which industries they should focus on. Finally, incorporating the recommendations into the already set economic development plan made in 2021 will significantly impact Baldwin City, Kansas.

REFERENCES

Baldwin City, KS. (2020). Retrieved from Data USA: https://datausa.io/profile/geo/baldwin-city-ks/

Goals for Baldwin City Economic Development Corp. (2021, January). Retrieved from Baldwincity.org: https://www.baldwincity.org/corecode/uploads/document/uploaded_pdfs/corecode/BCED%20Goals_213.pdf

Le, T. (2023, January). Educational Services in the US. Retrieved from IBIS World: https://my.ibisworld.com/us/en/industry/61/key-statistics

Morse, G. N., & Ha, I. (1997). How successful are business retention and expansion implementation efforts? Economic Development Review, 15(1), 8-13. Retrieved from proquest.com: https://bakeru.idm.oclc.org/login?url=https://www.proquest.com/scholarly-journals/how-successful-are-business-retention-expansion/docview/230088085/se-2

Osiobe, E. U. (2018, November 19). A local economic development action plan for Pennington County, South Dakota. Retrieved from Research Gate: https://www.researchgate.net/publication/329034384_A_Local_Economic_Development_Action_Plan_for_Pennington_County_South_Dakota

Thomas, B. (2023, April). Retail Trade in the US. Retrieved from IBIS World: https://my.ibisworld.com/us/en/industry/44-45/key-statistics Walker, D., & Hall, T. (2023). Business Retention & Expansion. Retrieved from purdue.edu: https://extension.purdue.edu/cdext/thematic-areas/community-economics-workforce-development/business-retention-expansion.html

Ejiro U. Osiobe

www.ingramcontent.com/pod-product-compliance
Lightning Source LLC
Chambersburg PA
CBHW030528210326
41597CB00013B/1068